GRADE
3

Common CORE Language

M000266971

Table of Contents

Common Core State Standards	Mini-Lessons and Practice Pages	Page
	Introduction	2
	Using This Book	3
Conventions of Standard English and Knowledge of Language		
	Lesson Plan Teacher Worksheet	4
L.3.1a	Nouns	6
L.3.1a	Pronouns	9
L.3.1a	Verbs	12
L.3.1a	Adjectives	15
L.3.1a	Adverbs	18
L.3.1b	Regular and Irregular Plural Nouns	22
L.3.1c	Use Abstract Nouns	30
L.3.1d	Regular and Irregular Verbs	34
L.3.1e	Simple Verb Tenses	42
L.3.1f	Subject–Verb and Pronoun–Antecedent Agreement	50
L.3.1g	Comparative and Superlative Adjectives and Adverbs	56
L.3.1h	Coordinating and Subordinating Conjunctions	64
L.3.1i	Produce Simple, Compound, and Complex Sentences	70
L.3.2a	Capitalize Words in Titles	78
L.3.2b	Commas in Addresses	82
L.3.2c	Commas and Quotation Marks in Dialogue	86
L.3.2d	Form and Use Possessives	90
L.3.2e	Use Conventional Spelling	94
L.3.2f	Use Spelling Patterns and Generalizations	100
L.3.2g	Use Reference Materials for Spelling	104
L.3.3a	Choose Words and Phrases for Effect	108
L.3.3b	Differences Between Spoken and Written Language	112
Vocabulary Acquisition and Use		
	Lesson Plan Teacher Worksheet	117
L.3.4a	Use Sentence-Level Context	118
L.3.4b	Affixes: Prefixes and Suffixes	122
L.3.4c	Root Words	128
L.3.4d	Use Glossaries or Dictionaries to Determine Meaning	132
L.3.5a	Distinguish Literal and Nonliteral Meanings	136
L.3.5b	Identify Real-Life Connections	140
L.3.5c	Shades of Meaning	144
Language Practice Assessments		
L.3.1–L.3.3	Conventions for Assessments	148
L.3.4–L.3.6	Assessments for Vocabulary	158
Answer Key		
	Practice Pages Answers	166
	Assessment Answers	179

Introduction

What Is the Common Core?

The Common Core State Standards are an initiative by states to set shared, consistent, and clear criteria for what students are expected to learn. This helps teachers and parents know what they need to do to help students. The standards are designed to be rigorous and pertinent to the real world. They reflect the knowledge and skills that young people need for success in college and careers.

If you teach in a state that has joined the Common Core State Standards Initiative, then you are required to incorporate these standards into your lesson plans. Students need targeted practice in order to meet grade-level standards and expectations, and thereby be promoted to the next grade.

What Does the Common Core Say About Language Standards?

In order for students to be college and career ready in language, they must gain control over many conventions of standard English grammar, usage, and mechanics as well as learn other ways to use language to convey meaning effectively.

Research shows that it is effective to use students' writing as a tool to integrate grammar practice. However, it is often hard to find a suitable context in which to teach such specific grade-level standards. Some students will need additional, explicit practice of certain skills. The mini-lessons and practice pages in this book will help them get the practice they need so they can apply the required skills during independent writing and on standardized assessments.

Students must also be proficient in vocabulary acquisition skills. This means being able to determine or clarify the meaning of grade-appropriate words. It also means being able to appreciate that words have nonliteral meanings, shades of meaning, and relationships to other words. These skills will enable students to read and comprehend rigorous informational texts and complex literary texts.

The Common Core State Standards state that the "inclusion of Language standards in their own strand should not be taken as an indication that skills related to conventions, effective language use, and vocabulary are unimportant to reading, writing, speaking, and listening; indeed, they are inseparable from such contexts."

Using This Book

Mini-Lessons and Practice Pages

Each grade-level volume in this series addresses all of the language standards for that grade. For each standard, three types of resources are provided that scaffold students using a gradual release model.

Based on your observations of students' language in writing and in collaborative conversations, choose mini-lessons that address their needs. The mini-lessons can be used during your literacy and writing block. Then use the practice pages to reinforce skills.

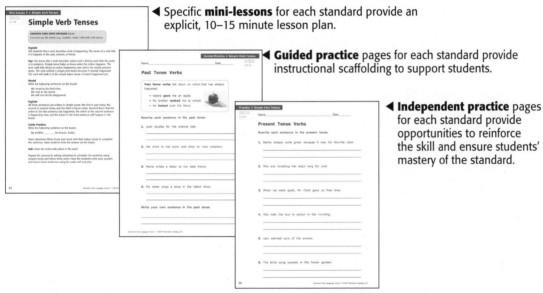

◀ Specific **mini-lessons** for each standard provide an explicit, 10–15 minute lesson plan.

▶ **Guided practice** pages for each standard provide instructional scaffolding to support students.

◀ **Independent practice** pages for each standard provide opportunities to reinforce the skill and ensure students' mastery of the standard.

Language Practice Assessments

Easy-to-use, flexible practice assessments for both Conventions and Vocabulary standards are provided in the last section of the book. The self-contained 2-page assessments cover skills in a reading passage format and have multiple choice answers.

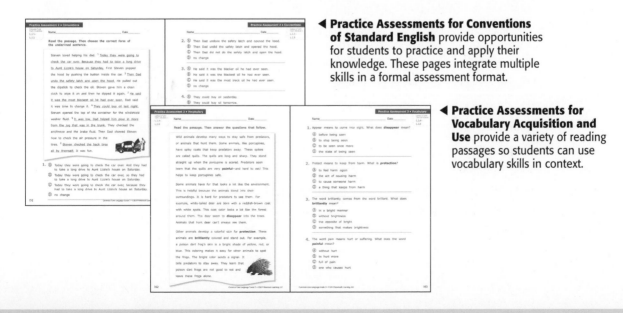

▶ **Practice Assessments for Conventions of Standard English** provide opportunities for students to practice and apply their knowledge. These pages integrate multiple skills in a formal assessment format.

◀ **Practice Assessments for Vocabulary Acquisition and Use** provide a variety of reading passages so students can use vocabulary skills in context.

Lesson Plan Teacher Worksheet
Conventions of Standard English and Knowledge of Language

The lessons in this section are organized in the same order as the Common Core Language Standards for conventions. Each mini-lesson provides specific, explicit instruction for a Language standard and is followed by multiple practice pages. Use the following chart to track the standards students have practiced. You may wish to revisit mini-lesson and practice pages a second time for spiral review.

Common Core State Standards	Mini-Lessons and Practice	Page	Complete (✓)	Review (✓)
L.3.1a	Mini-Lesson 1: Nouns	6		
	Practice Pages: Nouns	7		
L.3.1a	Mini-Lesson 2: Pronouns	9		
	Practice Pages: Pronouns	10		
L.3.1a	Mini-Lesson 3: Verbs	12		
	Practice Pages: Verbs	13		
L.3.1a	Mini-Lesson 4: Adjectives	15		
	Practice Pages: Adjectives	16		
L.3.1a	Mini-Lesson 5: Adverbs	18		
	Practice Pages: Adverbs	19		
L.3.1b	Mini-Lesson 6: Regular and Irregular Plural Nouns	22		
	Practice Pages: Regular and Irregular Plural Nouns	23		
L.3.1c	Mini-Lesson 7: Use Abstract Nouns	30		
	Practice Pages: Use Abstract Nouns	31		
L.3.1d	Mini-Lesson 8: Regular and Irregular Verbs	34		
	Practice Pages: Regular and Irregular Verbs	35		
L.3.1e	Mini-Lesson 9: Simple Verb Tenses	42		
	Practice Pages: Simple Verb Tenses	43		
L.3.1f	Mini-Lesson 10: Subject–Verb and Pronoun–Antecedent Agreement	50		
	Practice Pages: Subject–Verb and Pronoun–Antecedent Agreement	51		
L.3.1g	Mini-Lesson 11: Comparative and Superlative Adjectives and Adverbs	56		
	Practice Pages: Comparative and Superlative Adjectives and Adverbs	57		

(continued)

Common Core State Standards	Mini-Lessons and Practice	Page	Complete (✓)	Review (✓)
L.3.1h	Mini-Lesson 12: Coordinating and Subordinating Conjunctions	64		
	Practice Pages: Coordinating and Subordinating Conjunctions	65		
L.3.1i	Mini-Lesson 13: Produce Simple, Compound, and Complex Sentences	70		
	Practice Pages: Produce Simple, Compound, and Complex Sentences	71		
L.3.2a	Mini-Lesson 14: Capitalize Words in Titles	78		
	Practice Pages: Capitalize Words in Titles	79		
L.3.2b	Mini-Lesson 15: Commas in Addresses	82		
	Practice Pages: Commas in Addresses	83		
L.3.2c	Mini-Lesson 16: Commas and Quotation Marks in Dialogue	86		
	Practice Pages: Commas and Quotation Marks in Dialogue	87		
L.3.2d	Mini-Lesson 17: Form and Use Possessives	90		
	Practice Pages: Form and Use Possessives	91		
L.3.2e	Mini-Lesson 18: Use Conventional Spelling	94		
	Practice Pages: Use Conventional Spelling	95		
L.3.2f	Mini-Lesson 19: Use Spelling Patterns and Generalizations	100		
	Practice Pages: Use Spelling Patterns and Generalizations	101		
L.3.2g	Mini-Lesson 20: Use Reference Materials for Spelling	104		
	Practice Pages: Use Reference Materials for Spelling	105		
L.3.3a	Mini-Lesson 21: Choose Words and Phrases for Effect	108		
	Practice Pages: Choose Words and Phrases for Effect	109		
L.3.3b	Mini-Lesson 22: Differences Between Spoken and Written Language	112		
	Practice Pages: Differences Between Spoken and Written Language	113		
	Answer Keys	166		

COMMON CORE
STATE STANDARD

L.3.1a

Nouns

> **COMMON CORE STATE STANDARD L.3.1a**
> Explain the function of nouns, pronouns, verbs, adjectives, adverbs in general and their functions in particular sentences.

Explain
Tell students that a noun names a person, a place, or a thing.

Say: *A noun is a person, a place, or a thing. There are two types of nouns: common nouns and proper nouns. A common noun names any person, place, or thing. Examples of common nouns include* teacher, friend, country. *A proper noun names a particular person, place, or thing. A proper noun begins with a capital letter. A proper noun might be more than one word. Each word that is part of a proper noun will begin with a capital letter. Examples of proper nouns are* Aunt Terry, Canada, Jeffrey.

Model
Write these sentences on the board:

1. *My little sister played in the park.*
2. *Mia visited Aunt Helen in Florida.*
3. *Roger likes to attend the ballet.*

Underline the nouns in the examples. Point out that *sister* and *park* are nouns in the first sentence. *Sister* is a person, and *park* is a place. Point out that *Mia*, *Aunt Helen*, and *Florida* are nouns in the second sentence. *Mia* and *Aunt Helen* are people, and *Florida* is a place. These three nouns are proper nouns. Point out that *Roger* and *ballet* are nouns in the third sentence. *Roger* is a proper noun and *ballet* is a common noun.

Guide Practice
Write these sentences on the board. Ask a volunteer to underline the noun(s) in the first sentence.

1. *A bird sang in the tree.* (bird, tree)
2. *Beth lost her bracelet at the park.* (Beth, bracelet, park)
3. *The dog slept on the chair by the window.* (dog, chair, window)
4. *My grandfather likes to plant flowers.* (grandfather, flowers)
5. *The teacher gave the students a quiz.* (teacher, students, quiz)

Ask: *Did you underline the nouns?*

Repeat the procedure. Have the students find the nouns in each sentence. Remind them that a noun is a person, a place, or a thing.

Name_____ Date_____

Use Nouns

Nouns tell us the **person**, **place**, or **thing** in a sentence.

- **Mike** plays fetch with his **dog**. (person, thing)
- **Helen** picked **strawberries** with **Amber**. (person, thing, person)
- **Muhammad** rode his **bike** to the **park**. (person, thing, place)

Read each noun below. Write *person*, *place*, or *thing* on the line after the noun.

1. bike _____

2. library _____

3. Mr. Martin _____

4. beach _____

5. fish _____

6. United States _____

7. kangaroo _____

8. rock _____

9. Marybeth _____

10. police officer _____

COMMON CORE
STATE STANDARD

L.3.1a

Name_____ Date_____

Nouns

> A noun can be **common** or **proper**. **Proper nouns** are capitalized because they name specific people, places, and things. **Common nouns** are general and not capitalized.
>
> | Common Nouns | | Proper Nouns |
> |---|---|---|
> | ocean | | Atlantic Ocean |
> | park |  | Central Park |
> | zoo | | San Diego Zoo |

Underline the common noun(s) in each sentence.

1. My grandfather likes to plant flowers.

2. The teacher wrote her name on the chalkboard.

3. Liz likes to play the flute.

4. Mark has two fish in a bowl.

Underline the proper noun(s) in each sentence.

5. Mom parked the car in Uncle Hank's driveway.

6. Our dog Oreo wants Jess to throw the ball.

7. Dad's favorite restaurant is in Boston.

8. Leo lives in a city in Texas.

Common Core Language Grade 3 • ©2014 Newmark Learning, LLC

COMMON CORE
STATE STANDARD
L.3.1a

Pronouns

> **COMMON CORE STATE STANDARD L.3.1a**
> Explain the function of nouns, pronouns, verbs, adjectives, adverbs in general and their functions in particular sentences.

Explain
Tell students that a pronoun takes the place of a noun.

Say: *A pronoun takes the place of a noun. We use pronouns so we don't have to repeat the same noun over and over. Common pronouns include* I, me, you, he, she, him, her, it, its, they, them, their, us, our.

Model
Write these sentences on the board:

1. *Joey invited Fernando to his house for dinner.*
2. *Maria likes to cuddle with her cat Mr. Sparkles.*
3. *She went to the mall with her friends.*

Underline the pronouns in the examples. Point out that *his* is a pronoun in the first sentence that replaces the noun *Joey*. Point out that *her* is a pronoun in the second sentence that replaces the noun *Maria*. Point out that *She* and *her* are the pronouns in the third sentence.

Guide Practice
Write these sentences on the board. Ask a volunteer to circle the pronoun(s) in the first sentence.

1. *She walked to school with her sister.* (she, her)
2. *Dad made him paint the fence.* (him)
3. *Do you know where they went?* (you, they)
4. *Can you please give it to us?* (you, it, us)
5. *Mr. Rodriguez gave them homework.* (them)

Ask: *Did you circle the pronouns?*

Repeat the procedure with each sentence. Have the students find the pronouns in each sentence. Remind them that a pronoun replaces a noun, which is a person, a place, or a thing.

Common Core
State Standard

L.3.1a

Name_____ Date_____

Use Pronouns

A **pronoun** is a word that takes the place of one or more nouns. A pronoun must match the noun it replaces.

Singular Pronouns:

I, you, he, she, it, me, him, and *her*

Leo cleaned the kitchen.　　He cleaned it.

Plural Pronouns:

we, you, they, us, and *them*

Nicole and Joe read books.　　They read them.

Read the sentences. Choose a pronoun from the box that replaces the underlined section. Write it on the line.

them	it	They	She

1. Melissa loves to go sledding in the winter.

_____

2. Jack and Mike are cousins.

_____

3. The blue car is going to win the race.

_____

4. Emma and I paint pictures of trees.

_____

Name_____ Date_____

Pronouns

Rewrite each sentence using a pronoun in place of the underlined words. Words may need to be changed or removed.

1. The baby bird opened the <u>baby bird's</u> beak when the <u>baby bird's</u> mother flew into the nest.

_____

_____

2. My friend Angela wants to wear <u>Angela's</u> new coat to the football game tonight.

_____

_____

3. Nick and Tommy like to ride <u>Nick and Tommy's</u> bikes each day after school.

_____

_____

4. Mr. Antonio gave each of <u>Mr. Antonio's</u> students a box of crayons for an art project.

_____

_____

COMMON CORE
STATE STANDARD

L.3.1a

Verbs

> **COMMON CORE STATE STANDARD L.3.1a**
> Explain the function of nouns, pronouns, verbs, adjectives, adverbs in general and their functions in particular sentences.

Explain
Tell students that a verb either shows the action in a sentence or links other parts in a sentence.

Say: *Each sentence has at least one verb. Some verbs show the action in a sentence. These verbs are called action verbs. For example, in the sentence:* The horse jumped over the fence, *the verb is* jumped. *It describes an action.*

Some verbs link the parts of a sentence without describing the action. These verbs are called linking verbs. For example, in the sentence: Ms. Ross is my favorite teacher, *the verb is* is, *which links the subject to the pronoun* my.

Model
Write these sentences on the board:

1. *Katie kicked the ball.*
2. *The flowers are beautiful.*

Circle the verbs in the examples. Point out that *kicked* is the verb in the first sentence. It shows action. Point out that *are* is the verb in the last sentence. *Are* is a linking verb that links the subject *flowers* to the adjective *beautiful*.

Guide Practice
Write these sentences on the board. Ask volunteers to underline the verb in each sentence.

1. *The ducks swam across the pond.* (swam)
2. *The chicken soup smells delicious.* (smells)
3. *Jason sang a song in music class.* (sang)
4. *My sister drove us to school.* (drove)
5. *The dog is hungry.* (is)

Name_____ Date_____

Common Core
State Standard
L.3.1a

Use Verbs

A **verb** is a word that shows action. Verbs tell what the subject of the sentence does.

- Emily **baked** cupcakes for her friends.
- The fish **swim** upstream.
- Harold **asked** Mr. Titus a question.

Circle the verb or verbs in each sentence.

1. Amanda listened to the music.

2. The sea gull soared into the sky.

3. We play games every Saturday.

4. Tim laughs loudly whenever someone tells a joke.

5. A baby rabbit dashed across the lawn.

6. I eat lunch with my best friend every day.

7. The baby tigers wrestled with each other.

8. Dad cooked my favorite dinner for my birthday.

COMMON CORE
STATE STANDARD

L.3.1a

Name_____ Date_____

Verbs

Write a verb to complete each sentence.

1. The ice cream _____ good.

2. Brian and Sam _____ my best friends.

3. The dog _____ cute in that sweater.

4. The roses _____ nice.

5. My mother _____ happy whenever the sun shines.

6. Asa _____ sad that it is raining outside.

7. Bobby _____ to the end of the street.

8. The spaghetti _____ terrific.

9. Mrs. Miller _____ the song beautifully.

10. The boy _____ a hole in the sand.

Common Core Language Grade 3 • ©2014 Newmark Learning, LLC

Adjectives

COMMON CORE
STATE STANDARD
L.3.1a

> **COMMON CORE STATE STANDARD L.3.1a**
> Explain the function of nouns, pronouns, verbs, adjectives, adverbs in general and their functions in particular sentences.

Explain
Tell students that an adjective describes a noun and can tell how something looks, feels, tastes, smells, or sounds.

Say: *You know that an adjective is a descriptive word. It describes, or modifies, the noun in a sentence. It also tells how something looks, feels, tastes, smells, or sounds. For example, in the sentence:* Kelly has a brown horse named Chestnut, *the word* brown *is an adjective. It tells how the noun* horse *looks.*

Model
Write these sentences on the board:

1. *Peter played beautiful music on the piano.*
2. *A large, shaggy dog greeted us at the gate.*
3. *Molly made the spicy soup.*

Underline the adjectives in the examples. Point out that *beautiful* is an adjective in the first sentence. It describes the noun *music*. Point out that *large* and *shaggy* are adjectives in the second sentence that describe the noun *dog*. Point out *spicy* is an adjective in the last sentence. It describes the noun *soup*.

Guide Practice
Write these sentences on the board. Ask a volunteer to underline the adjective and circle the noun it modifies in the first sentence.

1. *The clear water sparkled in the sunshine.* (clear; water)
2. *Gina lives in a brick house.* (brick; house)
3. *The hot, sticky weather made us want to stay indoors.* (hot, sticky; weather)
4. *The sleek, black panther crept under the trees.* (sleek, black; panther)
5. *The tired baby cried.* (tired; baby)

Ask: *Did you underline the adjectives? Were you able to find the nouns that the adjectives modified?*

Repeat the procedure with each sentence. Have the students find the adjectives and the nouns they modify in each sentence. Remind them that an adjective describes a noun.

COMMON CORE
STATE STANDARD

L.3.1a

Name_____ Date_____

Use Adjectives

> **Adjectives** describe a noun and can tell how something **looks**, **feels**, **tastes**, **smells**, or **sounds**.
>
> - The <u>black</u> cat ran in our path.
> - Benny is <u>brown</u> with <u>white</u> spots.
> - Nana makes <u>tasty</u> <u>banana</u> bread.

Circle the adjectives in each sentence.
Underline the noun that the adjective describes.

1. The red bird perched at the top of the tree.

2. My lazy sister Ray likes to sleep until noon.

3. The boy with the black hair is Kevin.

4. The baby shook the rattle in its tiny hand.

5. Ask Paul to tell us a funny story.

6. We sat on a soft blanket because we did not want to sit on the wet grass.

7. The textbook for class was heavy.

8. The little dog played with his squeaky toy.

COMMON CORE
STATE STANDARD
L.3.1a

Name_____ Date_____

Adjectives

Fill in the chart below with four adjectives you would use to describe yourself.

Read the following paragraph and underline the adjectives.

Our hamster Charlie has long, curly fur. Charlie likes to sleep in the soft bedding in his large cage. When he is not napping, he likes to run in a big, purple wheel. He also likes to crawl through the long tunnels in his cage. As a special treat, we feed him juicy carrots and sweet cereal. Charlie is a wonderful pet.

COMMON CORE
STATE STANDARD

L.3.1a

Adverbs

> **COMMON CORE STATE STANDARD L.3.1a**
> Explain the function of nouns, pronouns, verbs, adjectives, adverbs in general and their functions in particular sentences.

Explain

Tell students that an adverb describes the how, when, and where of what is happening.

Say: *An adverb describes, or modifies, a verb. An adverb can also modify an adjective or even another adverb. Most adverbs are formed by adding -ly to an adjective. Some common adverbs include* chilly, gladly, high, quietly, slowly, softly, today, *and* very.

Model

Write these sentences on the board:

1. *Sam drew a picture of a flower carefully.*
2. *The stars shined brightly in the sky.*
3. *I am going to school today.*
4. *Put the bag there.*

Underline the adverbs in the examples. Point out the *-ly* ending for *carefully* and *brightly*. Point out that *carefully* answers the how of the verb *drew*. Point out that *brightly* answers the how of the verb *shined*. Point out that *today* answers the when of the verb *going*. Point out that *there* answers the where of the verb *put*.

Guide Practice

Write these sentences on the board. Ask a volunteer to underline the adverb in the first sentence and tell which question it answers.

1. *The birds flew high in the sky.* (high; where)
2. *The woman walked slowly up the street.* (slowly; how)
3. *They are going on a hike tomorrow.* (tomorrow; when)
4. *Franco ate the cereal nosily.* (nosily; how)
5. *Sally sang the hymn beautifully.* (beautifully; how)

Ask: *Did you underline the adverb? Does it describe the how, when, or where of what is happening in the sentence?*

Repeat the procedure with each sentence. Remind students that not all adverbs end in *-ly*.

Name_____ Date_____

Use Adverbs

> **Adverbs** tell us the **how**, **when**, or **where** of what is happening.
>
> - Amir runs down the steps **quickly**.
> - Our dog likes to play **outside**.
> - She had to get up **early** for work.

Circle the adverb and underline the verb that the adverb modifies in each sentence.

1. She looked at the bowl of fruit hungrily.

2. Phillip searched for his baseball mitt outside.

3. He rubbed his eyes sleepily.

4. Dad left for work early.

5. The door closed loudly.

6. Amy gently set the glass vase down on the table.

7. Ming filled his plate greedily with cookies.

8. They played games inside during the thunderstorm.

Common Core
State Standard

L.3.1a

Name_____ Date_____

Adverbs

Underline the adverb or adverbs in each sentence.

1. Mother danced with father gracefully.

2. Cassie wrote her name neatly on the line.

3. She let go of the balloon, and it flew high into the sky.

4. He hummed softly to the sleeping baby.

5. Please set the bowl carefully here.

6. The tiny flower grew steadily.

7. The child waited in line patiently.

8. They went inside because it was raining heavily.

9. I finished my homework first.

10. The cat knocked over the vase accidentally.

Name_____ Date_____

Nouns, Pronouns, Verbs, Adjectives, and Adverbs

Circle the nouns and underline the pronouns in each sentence.

1. Aaron went to the movies with his brother Phil.

2. My mom went to see a play in New York City.

3. Jacinda forgot to grab her purse when she left the house.

4. Ralph went upstairs, so he could play games with his brother.

5. The brothers walked to the bus stop around the corner, and they waited for the bus.

Underline the verb or verbs in each sentence.

6. Dad asked Daniel to wash his car.

7. My friend Nancy is thirsty.

8. Uncle Robert took us for ice cream.

9. The dog dug up the pretty sunflowers near the gate.

10. Rose placed the book on the shelf.

Underline the adjectives and circle the adverbs in the paragraph.

   The loud chef works in a busy restaurant nightly. The hot kitchen is very tiny. There is little room to move. Sometimes plates of hot food are dropped on the dirty floor accidentally. When this happens, the angry chef has to remake the delicious dishes.

COMMON CORE
STATE STANDARD

L.3.1b

Regular and Irregular Plural Nouns

> **COMMON CORE STATE STANDARD L.3.1b**
> Form and use frequently occurring regular and irregular plural nouns.

Explain

Remind students that some nouns have special endings when they name more than one person, place, or thing. Students must learn and remember the plural forms of irregular nouns. Write the word *tooth* on the board.

Say: *The rule for forming the plural of most nouns is to add -s or -es. But some nouns don't follow that rule. They have special plural forms. For these nouns, you must learn and remember the plural form. For example, some nouns spelled with a double* o *change to a double* e *in the plural form. The plural of* tooth *is* teeth. *The same is true for* goose *and* foot. *But other words, like* boot *and* hook, *are regular and just need an* -s *to make them plural.*

Say: *Some words that end in* -f, *like* elf, knife, *and* wolf, *also have a special plural form. The* -f *changes to a* -v, *so by adding* –es, *the plurals become* elves, knives, *and* wolves. *Other words, such as* roof *and* chief, *just need an* -s *to make them plural. That's why you have to remember the irregular nouns.*

Say: Shelf *is a noun that has a special plural form. When you talk about more than one shelf, do you say* shelfs *or* shelves? (shelves)

Model

Write the word pair *wife/wives* on the board. Point out the irregular plural form as you read the words aloud. Use the word in a sentence to model the plural form: *The wives are with their husbands.* Have students repeat the word to make sure they get the pronunciation right. Repeat for *leaf* and *scarf.*

Guide Practice

After you erase the plural forms from the board, ask the students to say them out loud. Offer prompts as necessary. When they have completed the list, work with the students to fill in the sentences below. Use the singular and irregular plural form of *elf*, *wolf*, and *goose*.

1. *The _____ ate dinner. (*elf, wolf, and goose)
2. *The _____ ate dinner. (*elves, wolves, and geese)

Have the students write the singular nouns *elf*, *wolf*, and *goose* in their journals. Then instruct them to write the plural form of each and use the plural noun in a sentence. Check their sentences to make sure they use the correct verb forms with each plural noun.

Name_____ Date_____

Regular Plural Nouns

A **regular plural noun** is a noun whose plural is formed by adding **-s** or **-es**. Here is how to tell what words need **-es**.

- Most words that end in **-ss**, **-ch**, **-sh**, **-x**, and **-z** need **-es** to form their plural.
- Some words that end in **-o**, such as *hero*, *tomato*, and *potato*, also need **-es** to become plural.

Words that need **-s**

spoon	**spoons**
pea	**peas**
wire	**wires**

Words that need **-es**

class	**classes**
wish	**wishes**
box	**boxes**

Write the correct plural form of each noun.

1. daughter _____

2. flash _____

3. patch _____

4. tomato _____

5. valley _____

6. buzz _____

7. flower _____

8. robe _____

9. telephone _____

10. hero _____

Common Core
State Standard

L.3.1b

Name_____ Date_____

Regular Plural Nouns

Underline the common noun or nouns in each sentence. Then write the plural form on the line.

1. We held the hammer by the handle.

_____

2. Rose won a ribbon in the race.

_____

3. Aunt Winn bought a box for the gift.

_____

4. The kitten chased the green bug.

_____

5. Robert's sister visited the beach.

_____

6. Henry put a sandwich on the table.

_____

7. Amy's rabbit lived in a wooden hutch.

_____

8. I had an egg and a potato for dinner.

_____

Common Core Language Grade 3 • ©2014 Newmark Learning, LLC

Name_____ Date_____

COMMON CORE
STATE STANDARD
L.3.1b

Regular Plural Nouns

**Change the noun to its plural form.
Then write a sentence using the plural noun.**

1. glass

_____

_____

2. brush

_____

_____

3. hero

_____

_____

4. turkey

_____

_____

5. fox

_____

_____

Common Core Language Grade 3 • ©2014 Newmark Learning, LLC

COMMON CORE
STATE STANDARD

L.3.1b

Name_____ Date_____

Form and Use Irregular Plural Nouns

> **Irregular plural nouns** name more than one thing but they require certain spelling changes.
>
> - For nouns that end in −**y** (but <u>not</u> −ey), change the −**y** to −**ies** to make the plural.
>
>   jur**y**   jur**ies**
>
> - Nouns that end in −**f** or −**fe** drop the −**f** and add −**ves** to become plurals.
>
>   shel**f**   shel**ves**

Write the correct plural form of the irregular nouns.

1. berry _____

2. life _____

3. pony _____

4. loaf _____

5. calf _____

6. sky _____

7. wife _____

8. strawberry _____

Common Core Language Grade 3 • ©2014 Newmark Learning, LLC

Name_____ Date_____

COMMON CORE
STATE STANDARD
L.3.1b

Form Irregular Plural Nouns

Change the underlined noun to its plural form. Then rewrite the sentence using the plural noun. You may have to change other words to make them match the plural nouns.

1. Jack believed he saw an <u>elf</u>.

_____

_____

2. The boy ran from the <u>wolf</u>.

_____

_____

3. The goose ate a <u>blueberry</u>.

_____

_____

4. Paki cut the <u>loaf</u> of bread with a <u>knife</u>.

_____

_____

5. Kara watched the horse lift its <u>hoof</u> for the blacksmith.

_____

_____

COMMON CORE
STATE STANDARD

L.3.1b

Name_____ Date_____

Use Irregular Plural Nouns

Change the noun to its plural form.
Then write a sentence using the plural noun.

1. shelf

_____

_____

2. thief

_____

_____

3. half

_____

_____

4. leaf

_____

_____

5. knife

_____

_____

Common Core Language Grade 3 • ©2014 Newmark Learning, LLC

COMMON CORE
STATE STANDARD
L.3.1b

Name_____ Date_____

Regular and Irregular Nouns

Change the regular and irregular nouns to make them plural.

1. donkey _____

2. life _____

3. juice _____

4. worm _____

5. fly _____

6. piano _____

7. spoon _____

8. princess _____

9. hoof _____

10. monkey _____

Write a sentence using each regular or irregular noun in its plural form.

1. foot

_____

_____

2. elf

_____

_____

3. cousin

_____

_____

4. sandwich

_____

_____

Use Abstract Nouns

> **Common Core Standard L.3.1c**
> Use abstract nouns (e.g., *childhood*).

Explain

Tell students that some nouns name concepts, attributes, and feelings.

Say: *Nouns name people, places, and things. We call these concrete nouns. Other nouns name things we can't see, smell, hear, taste, or touch. These concepts, attributes, and feelings are called abstract nouns. Concepts are ideas and attributes are features. Some common abstract nouns are* childhood, beauty, kindness, laughter, honesty, truth, anger, *and* sympathy.

Model

Write the following sentence on the board and point out the abstract noun *sympathy*.

> *We felt sympathy for the little girl whose balloon floated away.*

Guide Practice

Write the following sentences on the board:

1. *Milly admired the beauty of the fields and flowers.* (beauty)
2. *I remember my childhood as being imaginative and adventurous.* (childhood)
3. *His heart filled with dread when he saw the size of the other team.* (dread)

Ask a volunteer to circle the abstract noun in the first sentence.

Say: *Abstract nouns may not mean the same thing to everybody. Writers often explain their meanings by giving concrete examples.*

Point out that in the first example, the concrete words *fields* and *flowers* support the concept abstract noun *beauty*. Ask the volunteer to underline these support words. Repeat the process with the remaining sentences, asking the volunteers to find the abstract nouns.

Name_____ Date_____

COMMON CORE
STATE STANDARD
L.3.1c

Use Abstract Nouns

Abstract nouns are concepts or ideas, attributes or features, and feelings. These are things that cannot be heard, seen, smelled, tasted, or touched.

- **Childhood** is the best time of one's life.
- Your **generosity** will help the animal shelter.

Choose one abstract noun from each box and use it in a sentence.

beliefs	dreams	knowledge	culture

1. _I had 2 dreams last night._

success	courage	beauty	loyalty

2. _I had a grat success in my test._

love	sympathy	pride	sadness

3. _My Mom and Dad are in love._

COMMON CORE
STATE STANDARD
L.3.1c

Name_____ Date_____

Use Abstract Nouns

Write a sentence using each abstract noun.

1. friendship

_____

_____

2. anger

_____

_____

3. bravery

_____

_____

4. imagination

_____

_____

5. honesty

_____

_____

6. truth

_____

_____

Common Core Language Grade 3 • ©2014 Newmark Learning, LLC

Name_____ Date_____

COMMON CORE
STATE STANDARD
L.3.1c

Abstract Nouns

Complete each sentence. Think about the meaning of the italicized abstract noun.

1. Seek *knowledge* _____

_____

2. Life's simple *joys* _____

_____

3. The children felt *satisfaction* _____

_____

4. The puppy satisfied her *curiosity* _____

_____

Write two abstract nouns. Then use each one in a sentence.

5. _____

_____

6. _____

_____

COMMON CORE
STATE STANDARD

L.3.1d

Regular and Irregular Verbs

COMMON CORE STATE STANDARD L.3.1d
Form and use regular and irregular verbs.

Explain
Some verbs are regular but others are irregular.

Say: *Verbs are the action part of sentences. Sometimes the action is happening now, but sometimes it has happened in the past or will happen in the future. We can change the tense of many verbs easily by adding -d or -ed to make it past tense or the word* will *to make it future tense. These are regular verbs. Other verbs are called irregular verbs because they don't follow this pattern.*

Model
Write the following sentences on the board:

1. *We walk to the store.*
2. *We walked to the store.*
3. *We will walk to the store.*

4. *She is a good actress.*
5. *She was a good actress.*
6. *She will be a good actress.*

Point out the *-ed* ending of *walked* in the second sentence and the word *will* in the third sentence. Explain that *walk* is a regular verb. Point out the verbs and verb phrases in the fourth, fifth, and sixth sentences—*is*, *was*, and *will be*. Explain that *be* is an irregular verb—it does not follow the pattern to form past tense.

Guide Practice
Write the following regular verbs in a column on the board: *talk, tap,* and *wash*. Ask volunteers to come to the board to write the past tense of each verb (*talked, tapped, washed*). Point out the *-ed* ending on each word.

Write the following irregular verbs in a column on the board: *do, eat, fall, go, see,* and *sit*. Ask volunteers to come to the board to write the past tense of each verb (*did, ate, fell, went, saw, sat*). Point out the difference between regular and irregular past tense verbs: none of the irregular verbs take *-ed* endings.

Explain that the students must learn and remember the irregular verbs. They may need a dictionary to find the irregular verb forms.

 Common Core Language Grade 3 • ©2014 Newmark Learning, LLC

Name_____ Date_____

Regular Verbs

A verb in the **past tense** tells about an action that has already happened. Add **-ed** to most verbs in the past tense.

- If the verb ends with **-e**, just add **-d** to show past tense.

    tam**e**   tam**ed**

- If the verb ends with a consonant + **-y**, change **-y** to **-i** and add **-ed**.

    cr**y**   cri**ed**

- If a verb ends in a single vowel before the final consonant, double the final consonant and add **-ed**.

    dro**p**   dro**pped**

Write the correct past tense form of each verb.

1. watch _Watched_

2. beg _begged_

3. call _called_

4. drag _dragged_

5. carry _carried_

6. surprise _surprised_

7. drift _drifted_

8. poke _poked_

9. try _tried_

10. pick _picked_

COMMON CORE
STATE STANDARD
L.3.1d

Name_____ Date_____

Regular Verbs

**Write the correct past tense form of each verb.
Then use it in a sentence.**

1. float _____

_____

2. hug _____

_____

3. name _____

_____

4. poke _____

_____

5. push _____

_____

6. crawl _____

_____

Name_____ Date_____

Common Core
State Standard
L.3.1d

Regular Verbs

Write each sentence in the past tense.

1. I scrub my face every morning.

_____

2. The seeds sprout in the flowerpot.

_____

3. Beth passes the carrots at the dinner table.

_____

4. The plane lands on the runway.

_____

5. The ice melts on the sidewalk.

_____

6. Sandra boils the water and pours the tea.

_____

COMMON CORE
STATE STANDARD
L.3.1d

Name_____ Date_____

Irregular Verbs

> A verb in the **past tense** tells about an action that has already happened. **Irregular verbs** are not formed by following the pattern of adding **-d** or **-ed** to the end. You have to learn and remember them.

Use the words from the box to write the past tense form of each verb below.

blew	built	caught	chose	drank
gave	kept	led	left	lost
paid	read	rose	spread	stung
swam	swung	threw	wrote	made

1. choose _____

2. drink _____

3. keep _____

4. lose _____

5. catch _____

6. throw _____

7. give _____

8. rise _____

9. blow _____

10. build _____

11. write _____

12. read _____

13. swing _____

14. lead _____

15. make _____

16. leave _____

17. pay _____

18. spread _____

19. sting _____

20. swim _____

Name_____ Date_____

COMMON CORE
STATE STANDARD
L.3.1d

Irregular Verbs

Write the correct past tense form for each irregular verb.

1. spend _____

2. stand _____

3. do _____

4. drive _____

5. eat _____

6. pay _____

7. ride _____

8. take _____

9. shake _____

10. say _____

11. win _____

12. ride _____

13. wind _____

14. stick _____

15. see _____

16. break _____

COMMON CORE
STATE STANDARD
L.3.1d

Name_____ Date_____

Irregular Verbs Practice

Choose the correct past tense verb from the box to complete the sentences.

grew	left	stood	flew	fell	held

1. Hannah _____ so much that she needed bigger shoes.

2. I _____ my backpack on the bus yesterday.

3. Maria _____ on the porch waving goodbye.

4. The leaves in the yard _____ from the tree.

5. Mom always _____ my hand when we crossed the street.

6. The soccer ball _____ through the air and into the net.

Common Core Language Grade 3 • ©2014 Newmark Learning, LLC

Name_____ Date_____

Irregular Verbs Practice

**Write the correct past tense form of each verb.
Then use it in a sentence.**

1. eat _____

_____

2. sit _____

_____

3. hear _____

_____

4. pay _____

_____

5. ride _____

_____

6. drink _____

_____

COMMON CORE
STATE STANDARD
L.3.1e

Simple Verb Tenses

> **COMMON CORE STATE STANDARD L.3.1e**
> Form and use the simple (e.g., *I walked*; *I walk*; *I will walk*) verb tenses.

Explain

Tell students that a verb describes what is happening. The tense of a verb tells if it happens in the past, present, or future.

Say: *You know that a verb describes action and a linking verb links the parts of a sentence. Simple tense helps us know when the action happens. The verb* walk *tells about an action happening now and is the simple present tense. The verb* walked *is simple past tense because it already happened. The verb* will walk *is in the simple future tense—it hasn't happened yet.*

Model

Write the following sentences on the board:

1. *We raced to the finish line.*
2. *We race to the beach.*
3. *We will race to the playground.*

Explain

All three sentences are written in simple tense—the first in past tense, the second in present tense, and the third in future tense. Remind them that the action in the first sentence has happened, the action in the second sentence is happening now, and the action in the third sentence will happen in the future.

Guide Practice

Write the following sentence on the board:

My brother _____ his bicycle. (rode)

Have volunteers think of any past tense verb that makes sense to complete the sentence. Have students write the answer on the board.

Ask: *Does the action take place in the past?*

Repeat the process by asking volunteers to complete the sentence using present tense and future tense verbs. Have the students write past, present, and future tense sentences using the verbs *call* and *play*.

Name_____ Date_____

Past Tense Verbs

> **Past tense verbs** tell about an action that has already happened.
>
> - Valerie **gave** me an apple.
> - My brother **walked** me to school.
> - He **looked** over the fence.

Rewrite each sentence in the past tense.

1. Juan studies for the science test.

_____

_____

2. We drive to the store and shop for new sneakers.

_____

_____

3. Maria writes a letter to her best friend.

_____

_____

4. My sister sings a song in the talent show.

_____

_____

Write your own sentence in the past tense.

_____

_____

COMMON CORE
STATE STANDARD

L.3.1e

Name_____ Date_____

Past Tense Verbs

Rewrite the following paragraph in the past tense.

I hear a noise coming from the basement. I creep slowly down the stairs. I think it is just the washing machine, but I am really not sure. There is a big thumping noise. It repeats over and over. It sounds like a giant heartbeat. I reach the last step. I close my eyes and turn the corner. The thumping noise is getting louder. Then I laugh. I see my dog. He is standing next to the dryer and his wagging tail bangs against the dryer door.

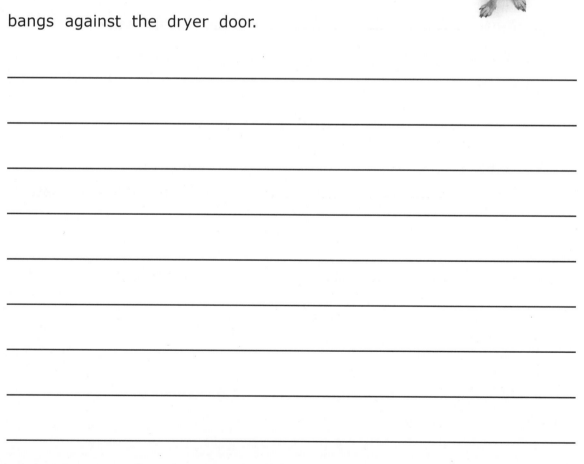

_____

_____

_____

_____

_____

_____

_____

_____

Name_____ Date_____

Present Tense Verbs

Present tense verbs tell what is happening now.

- Tina **climbs** the stairs.
- My cat **sleeps** in the window.
- She **is** the best student in third grade.
- Mario **seems** happy about the soccer game.

Read each sentence. Circle the correct present tense verb.

1. I _____ for my notebook.

        look   looked

2. Nora _____ the soup tastes salty.

        said   says

3. The ship _____ at the dock.

        waits   waited

4. David _____ the bus if he wakes up late.

        rides   will ride

5. He _____ very sleepy after dinner.

        got   gets

6. My dog _____ at everybody who goes by the house.

        barked   barks

COMMON CORE
STATE STANDARD
L.3.1e

Name_____ Date_____

Present Tense Verbs

Rewrite each sentence in the present tense.

1. Benny always wore green because it was his favorite color.

Benny always wearing green
because it was his favorite color.

2. Rita was brushing her dog's long fur coat.

Rita is brushing her dog long
fur coat.

3. When we were quiet, Mr. Clark gave us free time.

When we are quiet Mr. Clark
gives us free time.

4. She rode the bus to school in the morning.

She rids the bus to school
in the morning.

5. Lars seemed sure of the answer.

Lars seems sure of the answer.

6. The birds sung sweetly in the flower garden.

The birds sing sweetly in the
flower gordsh.

Name_____ Date_____

COMMON CORE
STATE STANDARD
L.3.1e

Future Tense Verbs

> **Future tense verbs** tell an action that is going to happen. To write about the future, use the special verb **will** in addition to the main verb.
>
> - The firefighter **will climb** the ladder.
> - Martina **will sleep** in the small tent.

Write each verb in the future tense.

1. picked, pick, _____Will pick_____

2. saw, see, _____Will see_____

3. watched, watch, _____Will watch_____

4. played, play, _____Will play_____

5. was, is, _____Will do_____

6. traveled, travel, _____Will travel_____

7. drove, drive, _____Will drive_____

8. left, leave, _____Will leave_____

9. drank, drink, _____Will drink_____

10. said, say, _____Will say_____

COMMON CORE
STATE STANDARD

L.3.1e

Name_____ Date_____

Future Tense Verbs

Rewrite each sentence in the future tense.

1. We cook dinner over a campfire.

_____

2. She returned her library books.

_____

3. Tita baked muffins for the children.

_____

4. He built a model plane.

_____

5. Saturday I cleaned my room.

_____

6. I went to the grocery store to get milk.

_____

Common Core Language Grade 3 • ©2014 Newmark Learning, LLC

Name_____ Date_____

Common Core
State Standard
L.3.1e

Simple Verb Tenses

Choose the correct verb tense for each sentence. Circle and write your answer.

1. Next week we _____ to my grandfather's house for his birthday.

      travel   will travel   traveled

2. We _____ our soccer game yesterday.

      win   will win   won

3. Let's _____ to the park now.

      go   went   will go

4. Last year Liza _____ in second grade.

      is   was   will be

5. They _____ the game about five minutes ago.

      will start   started   start

6. Please _____ here while I go into the store to pick up dinner.

      wait   waited   will wait

COMMON CORE
STATE STANDARD

L.3.1f

Subject–Verb and Pronoun–Antecedent Agreement

> **COMMON CORE STATE STANDARD L.3.1f**
> Ensure subject–verb and pronoun–antecedent agreement.

Explain
Subjects and verbs must agree. Pronouns and antecedents must also agree.

Say: *Nouns are persons, places, or things, and verbs are action words or linking words. Nouns and verbs must match, or agree, in number. Singular subjects require singular verbs, and plural subjects require plural verbs. Many singular verbs end in -s.*

Say: *The noun a pronoun replaces is called the antecedent. A pronoun and its antecedent must also match in number and gender.*

Model
Write the following sentence:

> *When butterflies _____ flowers butterflies sip nectar.*

Point out that the subject is plural and prompt the class to think of a possible verb. Point out the repeated subject, *butterflies*, and replace it with a pronoun.

Guide Practice
Write the following sentences:

1. *Martin _____ Martin's mother for a glass of water.* (asks; his)
2. *When a caterpillar _____ a caterpillar is hungry.* (hatches; it)

Ask a volunteer to write a verb that makes sense in the blank. Point out that the subject, *Martin*, is singular so the verb must be singular, too. Ask the volunteer to replace the second use of the subject with the correct pronoun.

Ask: *Does the verb agree with the subject in number? Does the pronoun agree with the antecedent in number and gender?*

Repeat the procedure with the remaining sentence. Point out that some sentences may contain more than one noun that can be replaced with a pronoun.

Name_____ Date_____

COMMON CORE
STATE STANDARD
L.3.1f

Subject–Verb Agreement

> The **subject** and **verb** in a sentence must agree in number.
>
> - Harry **wipes** his muddy sneakers on the mat.
> - Jane and I **wipe** the fog off the windows.

Circle the correct verb in each sentence.

1. Mittens (steal, steals) balls of yarn from Mother's basket.

2. Robins (hop, hops) across the grass in the spring.

3. Before we (eat, eats) we (wash, washes) our hands.

4. Beth (ask, asks) the police officer for directions.

5. They (wander, wanders) through the bookstore.

6. These trees (lose, loses) their leaves in the fall.

COMMON CORE
STATE STANDARD

L.3.1f

Name_____ Date_____

Subject–Verb Agreement

Complete each sentence by writing a verb that agrees with the subject.

1. The athlete _____ across the finish line.

2. My parents _____ tea after dinner.

3. Josiah and his brother _____ they are astronauts.

4. The alarm clock _____ me every morning.

5. Herman's canary _____ tunes.

6. My ice cream cone _____ sweet.

7. Pineapples _____ on large plantations.

8. The girls _____ skipping games.

9. The library _____ at 8 o'clock.

10. The softball team _____ after school.

Common Core Language Grade 3 • ©2014 Newmark Learning, LLC

Name_____ Date_____

COMMON CORE
STATE STANDARD
L.3.1f

Pronoun–Antecedent Agreement

> The **pronoun** and **antecedent** must agree in number and gender.
>
> - **Buster** barks when **he** wants a treat.
> - The **apples** are ripe when **they** turn red.
> - **We** turn in **our** uniforms after **our** last game.

Complete the sentences by writing the correct pronouns in the blank.

1. Horses are happy when _____ eat apples.

2. The girl smiled at _____ family in the audience.

3. Abraham Lincoln gave a speech when _____ visited Gettysburg.

4. We will be late if _____ luggage is lost.

5. The snails ate _____ lettuce.

6. Mindy asked if _____ could go to the fair.

7. Mr. Thomas stayed home because _____ was sick.

8. The astronaut put on _____ spacesuit.

COMMON CORE
STATE STANDARD

L.3.1f

Name_____ Date_____

Pronoun–Antecedent Agreement

Circle the correct pronoun(s) in each sentence.

1. A dozen kites danced, (its, their) tails waving madly.

2. The door swung slowly on (its, their) rusty hinges.

3. Nora giggled as (she, her) read (she, her) new book.

4. Will changed (his, its) shoes after practice.

5. Coach and I stood up as (we, they) watched the game.

6. When Robert arrived (he, his) threw open the door.

7. (I, Me) keep (my, mine) lunch money in the locker.

8. When spring returns, (its, it) will bring rain showers.

9. Sean called (his, her) parents after soccer practice.

10. The choir sang (their, they) best song.

11. The museum director loved (its, her) job.

12. Kevin and I watched (our, we) favorite action movie.

Name_____ Date_____

Common Core
State Standard
L.3.1f

Agreement

Choose the verb that agrees with the subject in each sentence.

1. The school of fish _____ between the rocks. (swim, swims)

2. My mother _____ classical music. (enjoy, enjoys)

3. We _____ better after working in the garden. (feel, feels)

4. The young couple _____ beside the lake. (walk, walks)

5. Ginger and Matthew _____ vegetables on the grill. (roast, roasts)

Choose the pronoun that agrees with the subject in each sentence.

6. Return the art supplies to _____ proper bins. (its, their)

7. Although I like this book, Julian finds _____ boring. (it, her)

8. Ricardo made posters and hung _____ in the windows. (it, them)

9. Each boy on the field tried _____ best to catch the baseball. (their, his)

10. Please sharpen the pencils if _____ are broken. (they, it)

COMMON CORE
STATE STANDARD

L.3.1g

Comparative and Superlative Adjectives and Adverbs

COMMON CORE STATE STANDARD L.3.1g

Form and use comparative and superlative adjectives and adverbs, and choose between them depending on what is to be modified.

Explain

Tell students that adjectives and adverbs modify, or change, other words. Comparative and superlative forms compare people, things, or actions.

Say: *You know that an adjective modifies a noun and an adverb modifies a verb, adjective, or other adverb. Adjectives and adverbs may do even more. Comparative adjectives compare two people, places, or things. Comparative adverbs compare the actions of two people, places, or things. Superlative adjectives compare three or more people, places, or things and superlative adverbs compare the actions of three or more people, places, or things.*

Model

Write these sentences on the board:

1. *Vince is fast.*
2. *Mary is faster.*
3. *Tomas is fastest.*
4. *June walked slowly.*
5. *Sara walked less slowly.*
6. *Jon walked least slowly.*

Point out the *-er* ending in the second sentence, which compares Mary's speed with Vince's speed. Explain that many adjectives and adverbs take the *-er* ending in their comparative forms. Point out the *-est* ending in the third sentence, which compares Tomas's speed with the others. Explain that many adjectives take the *-est* ending in their superlative forms. Point out the comparative and superlative forms in the fifth and sixth sentences. Explain that many adverbs take *more/most* or *less/least*. Some take irregular forms, however.

Guide Practice

Write the following words on the board: *high, wide, good, bad.* (*higher, highest; wider, widest; better, best; worse, worst*)

Ask volunteers to come to the board and write the comparative and superlative forms of the first word. Do they follow the *-er/-est* rule? Repeat the process with the remaining words. Do the adverbs follow the *more/most* and *less/least* rule? Explain that words such as *good* and *bad* take irregular comparative and superlative forms. Explain that these forms must be learned and may be found in a dictionary.

Common Core Language Grade 3 • ©2014 Newmark Learning, LLC

Name_____ Date_____

COMMON CORE
STATE STANDARD
L.3.1g

Form Comparative and Superlative Adjectives and Adverbs

Comparative forms of adjectives and adverbs compare two people or things.

> Molly was **faster** than Paul.

Superlative forms of adjectives and adverbs compare three or more people or things.

> Molly was the **fastest** on the team.

Circle the correct superlative form of each word.

1. good   most good, goodest, best

2. quickly   most quickly, quicker, quicklier

3. pretty   prettiest, more pretty, most pretty

4. dangerous   less dangerous, least dangerous, dangerousest

5. bad   worst, baddest, more bad

6. tall   taller, most tall, tallest

7. big   most big, bigger, biggest

8. happy   happiest, more happy, happier

COMMON CORE
STATE STANDARD

L.3.1g

Name_____ Date_____

Form Comparative and Superlative Adjectives

Write the comparative and superlative forms of each adjective.

		Comparative	Superlative
1.	green		
2.	open		
3.	beautiful		
4.	early		
5.	close		
6.	happy		
7.	fine		

Common Core Language Grade 3 • ©2014 Newmark Learning, LLC

Name_____ Date_____

COMMON CORE
STATE STANDARD
L.3.1g

Use Comparative and Superlative Adjectives

Write a sentence using the comparative form of each adjective.

1. tall

_____

2. hot

_____

3. high

_____

4. blue

_____

Write a sentence using the superlative form of each adjective.

5. low

_____

6. good

_____

7. bad

_____

8. happy

_____

COMMON CORE
STATE STANDARD
L.3.1g

Name_____ Date_____

Form Comparative and Superlative Adverbs

Comparative and superlative adverbs modify verbs, adjectives, or other adverbs.

- If an adverb has one syllable, add -ed for the comparative form. Add -est to form the superlative.

  high   high**er**   high**est**

- If an adverb has more than one syllable, add less or more to form the comparative. Add most or least to form the superlative.

  quickly   **more** quickly   **most** quickly

Read each sentence. Choose the correct comparative or superlative adverb from the box. Write it on the line.

more beautifully	most graceful	harder	farther	longest

1. My sister sang _____ than Katie did.

2. This science test was _____ than the last one.

3. Alaska is _____ away from me than California.

4. The ballerina in the pink is the _____ of all the ballerinas.

5. My hair is the _____ it has ever been!

Name_____ Date_____

COMMON CORE
STATE STANDARD
L.3.1g

Form Comparative and Superlative Adverbs

Write the comparative and superlative forms of each adverb.

		Comparative	Superlative
1.	sadly		
2.	slowly		
3.	quietly		
4.	warmly		
5.	far		
6.	soon		
7.	carefully		

Common Core
State Standard

L.3.1g

Name_____ Date_____

Use Comparative and Superlative Adverbs

Read each sentence. Underline the correct comparative or superlative adverb.

1. Children usually go to bed (earliest, earlier) than their parents.

2. The wolves growled (more ferociously, most ferociousy) than the dogs we brought with us.

3. The construction workers finished that building (more rapidly, most rapidly) than the last one.

4. She performed (better, best) of all the actors.

5. Lori speaks French (more correctly, most correctly) of all the students in our French class.

6. My mother goes to the grocery store (most frequently, more frequently) than my best friend's mother.

7. The championship soccer game was the (harder, hardest) game I have ever played.

8. My brother cleaned the house (more carefully, most carefully) than I did.

Common Core Language Grade 3 • ©2014 Newmark Learning, LLC

Name_____ Date_____

COMMON CORE
STATE STANDARD
L.3.1g

Choose Between Comparative and Superlative Adjectives and Adverbs

Place the following adjectives and adverbs in the correct box.

quieter	angrier	heavier	worst
shortest	fastest	simplest	shorter
easier	less	worse	prettier
least	best	better	simpler

comparative	superlative
_____	_____
_____	_____
_____	_____
_____	_____
_____	_____
_____	_____
_____	_____
_____	_____

COMMON CORE
STATE STANDARD

L.3.1h

Coordinating and Subordinating Conjunctions

COMMON CORE STATE STANDARD L.3.1h
Use coordinating and subordinating conjunctions.

Explain

Tell students that coordinating and subordinating conjunctions can be used to form compound and complex sentences.

Say: *Sometimes we want to join independent clauses to make compound sentences. We can use coordinating conjunctions—and, but, or, for, nor, so, and yet. We can also use subordinating conjunctions to introduce a dependent clause, which is a part of a sentence that can't stand alone.*

Model

Write the following sentences on the board:

1. *We planned a picnic at the park. It started to rain.*
2. *We have only six bananas. Seven children are asking for fruit.*

Show students how to create a compound sentence out of the first sentence pair by using the conjunction *but.* (*We planned a picnic at the park, but it started to rain.*) Point out the placement of the comma before the connecting word. Show the students how to use the subordinating conjunction *although* to make a complex sentence using the second sentence pair. (*Although we have only six bananas, seven children are asking for fruit.*)

Guide Practice

Write the following sentences on the board:

1. *Jon washed his bicycle. He went for a ride around the block.*
   (Jon washed his bicycle, and he went for a ride around the block.)
2. *I went to lunch. I wasn't hungry.* (I went to lunch, but I wasn't hungry.)

Ask a volunteer to create a compound sentence using the first pair of sentences.

Ask: *Which conjunction best fits the ideas of the sentence pairs? How do you create the complex sentence? What do you remove and what do you change?*

Repeat the procedure with the remaining sentences.

Name_____ Date_____

COMMON CORE
STATE STANDARD
L.3.1h

Coordinating Conjunctions

> Join simple sentences to make compound sentences using coordinating conjunctions. Common conjunctions are: *and, but, or, for, nor, so, yet.*
>
> - Kim doesn't enjoy jumping, **but** she often skips rope.
> - I could go swimming, **or** I could go hiking.

Use coordinating conjunctions to combine the following pairs of sentences. Write the new sentence on the line.

1. I can't go to the pool today. I can't go to the pool tomorrow.

_____

_____

2. Should Gina buy a juice? Should she eat an orange?

_____

_____

3. My sister wants to see a movie. She will buy a paper to

check the show times.

_____

_____

COMMON CORE
STATE STANDARD

L.3.1h

Name_____ Date_____

Coordinating Conjunctions

Use the following sentence pairs to create a compound sentence. Underline the coordinating conjunction in each new sentence.

1. Will the game end in a tie? Will it go into overtime?

_____

_____

2. The cake looked beautiful. Few people ate it.

_____

_____

3. The snow stopped falling. We took our sleds outside.

_____

_____

4. Gina measured the flour. Her mother cracked the eggs.

_____

_____

5. Dad couldn't find his keys. Mom found them in his jacket pocket.

_____

_____

6. I had a science test. I studied.

_____

_____

Name_____ Date_____

COMMON CORE
STATE STANDARD
L.3.1h

Subordinating Conjunctions

Join **independent** and **dependent** clauses to form complex sentences using **subordinating conjunctions**. Commas are usually used following the dependent clause when it is at the beginning of a sentence.

- The game was on TV **until** the power went out.
- **Because** we got lost, we missed the show.

Combine the following pairs of sentences using subordinating conjunctions from the box. Write the new sentence on the line.

however	after	when	because	where

1. I will pick you up at 5 o'clock. I might be late.

_____

_____

2. We climbed the stairs. We found an artist painting at the window.

_____

_____

3. Ingrid heard the buzzer. She went to the door.

_____

_____

COMMON CORE
STATE STANDARD

L.3.1h

Name_____ Date_____

Subordinating Conjunctions

Choose six subordinating conjunctions from the list. Write a sentence with each one and underline the subordinating conjunctions.

after	although	as	because	which
before	even though	if	rather than	while
since	that	though	unless	even
when	where	whether	until	

1. _____

_____

2. _____

_____

3. _____

_____

4. _____

_____

5. _____

_____

6. _____

_____

Common Core Language Grade 3 • ©2014 Newmark Learning, LLC

Name_____ Date_____

COMMON CORE
STATE STANDARD
L.3.1h

Coordinating and Subordinating Conjunctions

Write three sentences using coordinating conjunctions.

1. _____

_____

2. _____

_____

3. _____

_____

Write three sentences using subordinating conjunctions.

4. _____

_____

5. _____

_____

6. _____

_____

COMMON CORE
STATE STANDARD

L.3.1i

Produce Simple, Compound, and Complex Sentences

> **COMMON CORE STATE STANDARD L.3.1i**
> Produce simple, compound, and complex sentences.

Explain
Tell students how to write simple, compound, and complex sentences.

Say: *A sentence contains a subject and a predicate. The subject is the "who" or "what" of the sentence. The predicate is the action that the subject does. A simple sentence is made up of subjects and predicates. Sometimes simple sentences have more than one subject or predicate. Simple sentences also have one independent clause, which is a complete sentence with a subject and verb.*

A compound sentence has two or more simple sentences, or independent clauses, joined by a coordinating conjunction, such as: and, but, or, so, yet.

A complex sentence has one independent clause and one or more dependent clauses. A dependent clause is not a complete sentence, but it does have a subject and a verb. A dependent clause sometimes begins with one of the following words: after, although, as, as if, because, before, if, since, though, unless, until, whatever, when, whenever, whether, *and* while.

Model
Write the following sentences on the board:

1. *He ran in the race.*
2. *I ate my breakfast, and I went to school.*
3. *When the movie ended, the students clapped.*

The first sentence is simple. Point out that it contains a subject and a predicate and is an independent clause. The second sentence is compound. Point out that it contains two independent clauses linked by the conjunction *and*. The third sentence is complex. Point out that it contains an independent clause and a dependent clause. It starts with the hint word *When*.

Guide Practice
Write the following sentences on the board. Ask students to identify them as simple, compound, or complex.

1. *I didn't eat the sandwich because I don't like tuna salad.* (complex)
2. *Lee sneezed, and he blew his nose.* (compound)
3. *School ends at three o'clock.* (simple)

Name_____ Date_____

COMMON CORE
STATE STANDARD
L.3.1i

Produce Simple Sentences

All sentences have a **subject** and a **predicate**.
The subject is the "who" or "what" of the sentence.
The predicate is the action that the subject does.

<u>Marta and Myron</u> <u>play the piano for their grandmother</u>.
(subject)   (predicate)

Read the words below. Put a check mark next to the words that form a complete sentence.

1. ☐ ate a sandwich

2. ☐ the insect built a nest

3. ☐ the mechanic changed the oil in the car

4. ☐ the doctor

5. ☐ walks to the bus stop with Phillip

6. ☐ placed the stamp on the letter

7. ☐ the boat sailed

8. ☐ a little chick pecked at the food

COMMON CORE
STATE STANDARD

L.3.1i

Name_____ Date_____

Produce Simple Sentences

Circle the subject and underline the predicate in each sentence.

1. Mother passed the salt to father.

2. Tyrell makes funny faces in the mirror.

3. The plane landed smoothly on the runway.

4. The hawk soars high in the clear sky.

5. The pirate buried the treasure.

Write a simple sentence using the provided subjects and predicates.

6. canary

_____

_____

7. Christina

_____

_____

8. studied for the test.

_____

_____

9. went down the water slide.

_____

_____

Common Core Language Grade 3 • ©2014 Newmark Learning, LLC

COMMON CORE
STATE STANDARD
L.3.1i

Name_____ Date_____

Produce Compound Sentences

A **compound sentence** is made up of two or more simple sentences that are linked by a comma and a conjunction.

- The leaf fell off the tree, **and** it landed on the ground.
- The pillow is firm, **but** the bed is soft.
- The tube is made of rubber, **so** it can bend easily.

Combine the following pairs of simple sentences into a compound sentence, using the conjunctions *and*, *but*, **or** *or*.

1. I brushed my teeth. I went to bed.

_____

_____

2. Manny likes fruit pie. Rita likes cream pie.

_____

_____

3. Do you want to watch a movie? Do you want to play outside?

_____

_____

4. The hammer is used to hit nails. The ax is used to chop wood.

_____

_____

COMMON CORE
STATE STANDARD

L.3.1i

Name_____ Date_____

Produce Compound Sentences

Circle the subjects and underline the predicates in each sentence.

1. The leaves change colors, and they fall off the trees in autumn.

2. Julie packed her suitcase, and she flew on a plane.

3. Orange is my favorite color, but yellow is my least favorite color.

4. The boys cleaned the garage, so Dad took them to the park.

5. The class went to the zoo, and they learned about different animals.

Write a compound sentence about what you did today.

_____

_____

_____

Write a compound sentence about what you will do tomorrow.

_____

_____

_____

Name_____ Date_____

COMMON CORE
STATE STANDARD
L.3.1i

Produce Complex Sentences

A **complex sentence** is made up of one simple sentence (independent clause), and one incomplete sentence (dependent clause). The dependent clause is not a complete thought, so it needs the independent clause to make a complete sentence.

- The noise hurt my ears because it was loud.
  (independent clause)   (dependent clause)

- When the president arrives, the city will block the streets.
  (dependent clause)   (independent clause)

Underline the dependent clauses in each sentence.

1. Cal likes the ocean, although he does not know how to swim.

2. Even though the necklace is pretty, she wanted a bracelet instead.

3. After the chef added the flour, he mixed the ingredients.

4. They will jump out and yell "surprise" when Ted opens the door.

5. The boy wore a life vest because they were going sailing.

6. After the farmer plowed the fields, he fed the hungry horses.

COMMON CORE
STATE STANDARD

L.3.1i

Name_____ Date_____

Produce Complex Sentences

Circle the independent clauses in each sentence.

1. Even though it is raining, the sun is in the sky.

2. Susie yelled at her little sister because she borrowed her book without asking.

3. Before Mr. Brecker dismissed class, he gave out homework.

4. David's mom drove him to school since he missed the bus.

5. Although she plays on the soccer team, she also enjoys basketball.

Write a simple sentence.

_____

_____

_____

Write a compound sentence.

_____

_____

_____

Write a complex sentence.

_____

_____

_____

Name_____ Date_____

Common Core
State Standard
L.3.1i

Produce Simple, Compound, and Complex Sentences

Read the following sentences and write if it is simple, compound, or complex.

1. Canada is located in North America. _____

2. Although she didn't want to sleep in a tent, Bea still wanted to go camping. _____

3. The sky was a shade of deep blue, and the clouds looked like cotton balls. _____

4. After the family ate dinner, they went for a long walk in the park. _____

5. The bird gathered pieces of straw to build a nest.

_____

6. The children drew on the sidewalk with colorful chalk, so they could play a game of hopscotch. _____

7. Mark washed the dishes, even though it was his brother's turn. _____

8. Before Claudia went outside, she put on her coat, hat, and gloves. _____

9. The wolf huffed and puffed. _____

10. The deer ran across the meadow, and the rabbit bounced behind it. _____

COMMON CORE
STATE STANDARD

L.3.2a

Capitalize Words in Titles

> **COMMON CORE STATE STANDARD L.3.2a**
> Capitalize appropriate words in titles.

Explain

Tell students how to recognize the correct words to capitalize in titles of books and movies.

Say: *You know that certain words should be capitalized in sentences. In titles the first word, the last word, and almost every word in between* (nouns, pronouns, verbs, adjectives, adverbs) *should be capitalized. Do not capitalize articles* (a, an, the). *Do not capitalize short prepositions* (as, by, for, in, of, on, to). *Do not capitalize conjunctions* (and, but, or, nor). *Capitalize the first word in the subtitle of a title. A subtitle comes after a colon. Look at this title* The Cat in the Hat. *The words* The, Cat, *and* Hat *are capitalized. The word* in *is not because it is a short preposition, and the word* the *is not because it is an article.*

Model

Write these titles on the board:

1. *The Pokey Little Puppy*
2. *A Bug's Life*
3. *The Chronicles of Narnia: The Lion, the Witch, and the Wardrobe*

In the first and second titles, all of the words should be capitalized. Point out that the words should all be capitalized because they follow the rules. In the last title, the words *The, Chronicles, Narnia, The, Lion, Witch,* and *Wardrobe* should be capitalized. The second *The* should be capitalized because it is the first word in a subtitle. The words *of, the, and,* and *the* should not be capitalized. The first and last words and most words in between should be capitalized in titles.

Guide Practice

Write these titles on the board. Ask volunteers to circle each word that should be capitalized.

1. *the adventures of milo and otis* (The Adventures of Milo and Otis)
2. *black beauty* (Black Beauty)
3. *little house in the big woods* (Little House in the Big Woods)
4. *the velveteen rabbit* (The Velveteen Rabbit)
5. *charlotte's web* (Charlotte's Web)

Ask: *Did you circle the correct words that need to be capitalized?*
Repeat the procedure with each sentence.

COMMON CORE
STATE STANDARD
L.3.2a

Name_____ Date_____

Capitalize Words in Titles

When writing **titles**, **capitalize** the first word, the last word, and almost every word in between.
Do not capitalize certain short words in between such as articles, prepositions, and conjunctions.

- **P**ippi **L**ongstocking
- **C**harlie and the **C**hocolate **F**actory
- **J**ames and the **G**iant **P**each

Write each title correctly on the line.

1. tales of a fourth grade nothing

_____

2. the legend of sleepy hollow

_____

3. the wonderful wizard of oz

_____

4. the adventures of tom sawyer

_____

5. anne of green gables

_____

6. a wrinkle in time

_____

Common Core
State Standard
L.3.2a

Name_____ Date_____

Capitalize Words in Titles

**Underline the title in each sentence.
Then write it correctly underneath.**

1. Through the looking-glass is about the adventures of a little girl named Alice.

_____

2. Actor Robin Williams stars in mrs. doubtfire, which is my favorite movie.

_____

3. My favorite book of the Harry Potter series is harry potter and the chamber of secrets.

_____

4. I learned about owls and hawks by reading thunder birds: nature's flying predators.

_____

5. I enjoyed the movie kit kittredge: an american girl.

_____

Common Core Language Grade 3 • ©2014 Newmark Learning, LLC

Name_____ Date_____

COMMON CORE
STATE STANDARD
L.3.2a

Capitalize Words in Titles

Choose the title that is capitalized correctly.

1. Ⓐ Where the wild things are

   Ⓑ where The Wild Things are

   Ⓒ Where the Wild Things Are

2. Ⓐ The wind In The willows

   Ⓑ The Wind in the Willows

   Ⓒ The Wind In The Willows

3. Ⓐ the phantom tollbooth

   Ⓑ The phantom Tollbooth

   Ⓒ The Phantom Tollbooth

4. Ⓐ The Little Engine That Could

   Ⓑ The little engine that could

   Ⓒ The Little Engine that Could

5. Ⓐ What do You do with a Tail like This?

   Ⓑ What Do You Do with a Tail Like This?

   Ⓒ What Do You Do With A Tail Like This?

6. Ⓐ The sword in The Stone

   Ⓑ The Sword in the Stone

   Ⓒ the Sword in the stone

COMMON CORE
STATE STANDARD
L.3.2b

Commas in Addresses

> **COMMON CORE STATE STANDARD L.3.2b**
> Use commas in addresses.

Explain
Tell students the correct placement of commas in addresses.

Say: *Commas are used to set off items in sentences. In addresses, commas are also used to set off different parts of the address. Place a comma after the name, street address, city, and state. A comma is not needed between a state and a ZIP code. If just a city and state are used, place a comma between the city and state, if it appears within a sentence.*

Model
Write these addresses on the board:

1. *Judy Garcia 1255, Harper Road, Lexington, KY, 40502*
2. *Judy Garcia, 1255 Harper Road, Lexington, KY 40502*
3. *Judy Garcia, 1255 Harper Road, Lexington KY, 40502*

Point out that the commas should be placed between the name line and the address, the address and the city, and the city and the state. The second choice is correct.

Guide Practice
Write the following on the board. Ask a volunteer to place the commas in the correct places.

1. *Randall Johnson 10 Second Street New York NY 10453*
   (set commas after Johnson, Street, and York)
2. *He was born in Pittston Pennsylvania in 1979.*
   (set commas after Pittston and Pennsylvania)
3. *Mimi Rogers 43 Crestfallen Lane Boise ID 83701*
   (set commas after Rogers, Lane, and Boise)

Ask: *Did you place the commas in the correct places?*

Repeat the procedure with each sentence. Have the students place the commas in the correct spots. Remind them that a comma is not needed between a state and a ZIP code.

Name_____ Date_____

COMMON CORE
STATE STANDARD
L.3.2b

Use Commas in Addresses

In **addresses** commas are used to set off the name line from the address line, the address line from the city, and the city from the state.

- Wendy Jin, 4004 New Street, Duryea, PA 18642
- Hector White, 9996 Pine Court, Santa Fe, NM 87501
- Vito Shara, 555 West Avenue NW, Houston, TX 77008

Read each address. Check the box if the commas are in the correct places.

1. ☐ World Wildlife Fund, 1250 24th Street, NW, Washington, DC, 20090

2. ☐ Betsey Phillips, 679 Johnson Way, Seattle WA, 98101

3. ☐ Jeremy Frederick, 444 Lioness Street, New Haven, CT 60511

4. ☐ Walter Sanchez, 2, 4th Avenue, Minot ND, 58703

5. ☐ National Park Service, 240 West 5th Avenue, Suite 114, Anchorage, AK 99501

COMMON CORE
STATE STANDARD
L.3.2b

Name_____ Date_____

Use Commas in Addresses

Place the comma or commas in the correct places.

1. My brother attends Harvard University in Cambridge Massachusetts.

2. William Getty 33 Juniper Place Detroit MI 48201

3. Regina Herman 60511 Station Boulevard Biloxi MS 39530

4. Kareem Greene 888 Whispering Pines Lane Saint Paul MN 55104

5. I want to go on vacation in San Francisco California.

6. Uncle Arthur likes to fish in Sitka Alaska in the winter months.

7. Jessica Lewis-Day 75 North Red Rock Street Denver CO 80022

8. The beaches in Cape May New Jersey are beautiful.

Common Core Language Grade 3 • ©2014 Newmark Learning, LLC

Name_____ Date_____

COMMON CORE
STATE STANDARD
L.3.2b

Use Commas in Addresses

Choose the address with the commas in the correct places.

1. Ⓐ Bill Curren, 7632 Overland Road, Las Vegas, NV 89101

   Ⓑ Bill Curren, 7632, Overland Road, Las, Vegas, NV, 89101

   Ⓒ Bill Curren, 7632 Overland Road Las Vegas, NV, 89101

2. Ⓐ Francine Harper, 92 Betty Lane, Nashville, TN, 37213

   Ⓑ Francine Harper 92 Betty, Lane, Nashville, TN, 37213

   Ⓒ Francine Harper, 92 Betty Lane, Nashville, TN 37213

3. Ⓐ Ernesto Butler, 349966 Mockingbird Alley, Akron OH 44303

   Ⓑ Ernesto Butler 349966, Mockingbird Alley, Akron OH, 44303

   Ⓒ Ernesto Butler, 349966 Mockingbird Alley, Akron, OH 44303

4. Ⓐ Margaret Wilford, 26, Eleventh Street, Chicago, IL, 60007

   Ⓑ Margaret Wilford, 26 Eleventh Street, Chicago, IL 60007

   Ⓒ Margaret Wilford 26, Eleventh, Street Chicago, IL 60007

5. Ⓐ Oscar Capote, 2316, Gotham Road, New York, NY, 10021

   Ⓑ Oscar Capote, 2316 Gotham Road, New York, NY 10021

   Ⓒ Oscar Capote, 2316 Gotham Road New York, NY 10021

COMMON CORE
STATE STANDARD
L.3.2c

Commas and Quotation Marks in Dialogue

> **COMMON CORE STATE STANDARD L.3.2c**
> Use commas and quotation marks in dialogue.

Explain
Tell students the correct placement of commas and quotation marks in dialogue.

Say: *In dialogue, which is a conversation, commas are used to set off the speaker's words from the rest of the sentence. Quotation marks are used to show the speaker's words exactly as they were spoken. A comma is placed before the quotation. Quotation marks are placed around the dialogue. Punctuation—periods, exclamation marks, question marks, and commas—go inside quotation marks.*

Model
Write the following sentences on the board:

1. *This is the best day of my life! he said.*
2. *The weatherman said It looks like it will rain tonight.*

Place quotation marks around the dialogue in the sentences. Point out that the quotation marks should come before *This* and after the exclamation point (!) in the first sentence. The quotation marks should come before *It* and after the period at the end of the second sentence.

Guide Practice
Write these sentences on the board. Ask a volunteer to place the commas in the correct places.

1. *"Please set the table" she told the children.* (set comma after table)
2. *Eli asked his friend Jamir "Do you want to eat dinner at my house? My mom said it is okay."* (set comma after Jamir)
3. *Nancy swore me to secrecy and said "I don't want anyone to know."* (set comma after said)

Ask: *Did you place the commas in the correct places?*

Repeat the procedure with each sentence. Have the students place the commas in the correct spots. Remind them that a comma is used to set off the dialogue from the rest of the text.

Common Core Language Grade 3 • ©2014 Newmark Learning, LLC

Name_____ Date_____

COMMON CORE
STATE STANDARD
L.3.2c

Use Commas and Quotation Marks in Dialogue

> In dialogue **commas** are used to set off the speaker's words from the rest of the sentence. **Quotation marks** are used to show what the speaker's exact words are.
>
> - Kaitlyn told her brother, "Count to ten while I go find a place to hide."
> - "I'm proud of the way you played today," the coach said to the soccer players.

Choose the sentence with the commas and quotations marks in the correct places.

1. Ⓐ The server asked the table of people, "Will that be all today?"

   Ⓑ The server, asked the table of people, "Will that be all today?"

   Ⓒ "The server asked the table of people," Will that be all today?

2. Ⓐ I want to be a firefighter like my dad when I grow up, "Carlos said to the class."

   Ⓑ "I want to be a firefighter like my dad when I grow up, Carlos said to the class."

   Ⓒ "I want to be a firefighter like my dad when I grow up," Carlos said to the class.

3. Ⓐ Joy exclaimed to her sister, "I got the job!"

   Ⓑ Joy exclaimed, "to her sister I got the job!"

   Ⓒ "Joy exclaimed to her sister, I got the job!"

COMMON CORE
STATE STANDARD

L.3.2c

Name_____ Date_____

Use Quotation Marks in Dialogue

Read each sentence and place the quotation marks in the correct spot.

1. The excited boy yelled to his grandmother, I see it! I see it!

2. The babysitter said to the children, Who wants to go to the park today?

3. It won't be too much longer now until the doctor will see you, said the nurse to the patient.

4. Alice nervously recited from the stage, Jack and Jill went up the hill.

5. He picked up the phone and said, Hello. This is Mr. Weaver. How can I help you?

6. She looked at her sister and asked, Are you wearing my shirt to school today?

7. My mom gave me a big hug and said, You were so great in the play! I am so proud.

8. What would you like for dinner tonight? my dad asked.

Name_____ Date_____

COMMON CORE
STATE STANDARD
L.3.2c

Use Commas and Quotation Marks in Dialogue

Read each sentence and place the comma and quotation marks in the correct spots.

1. The doctor asked the little girl How are you feeling?

2. She sang the lyrics You are my sunshine, my only sunshine.

3. Hurry along, and have a safe day the crossing guard said to the students.

4. You have a choice between salad and broccoli today said the lunch lady to the hungry little boy.

5. Mr. White asked Who is ready for a pop quiz?

Write a sentence using a comma and quotation marks.

_____

_____

_____

_____

COMMON CORE
STATE STANDARD
L.3.2d

Form and Use Possessives

> **COMMON CORE STATE STANDARD L.3.2d**
> Form and use possessives.

Explain
Tell students that possessive forms of nouns show that something belongs to a person, place, or thing.

Say: *Nouns are people, places, or things. Some nouns show that something belongs to one or more people, places, or things. These are called possessives. We use an apostrophe followed by an -s to show that singular and most irregular plural nouns are possessive. We add an apostrophe -s even if the possessive noun ends in an -s. We use an apostrophe after the -s to make a regular plural noun possessive.*

Model
Write these sentences on the board:

1. *The boy's shirt is red.*
2. *The boys' shirts are red.*
3. *The children's shirts are red.*

Point out the position of the apostrophe in each sentence. The first sentence describes a singular possessive—the shirt of the boy. The second sentence describes a plural possessive—the shirts of the boys. Point out the *'s* in the third sentence—the shirts of the children. Because *children* is a collective noun, it is treated as a singular noun when forming the possessive.

Guide Practice
Write the following phrases on the board:

1. *the hat of the man* (the man's hat)
2. *the baby of the couple* (the couple's baby)
3. *the shoes of Tomas* (Tomas's shoes)

Ask a volunteer to write the possessive form of the first phrase on the board.

Ask: *What is the possessive noun, or the owner of the object?* (man) *Is it singular or plural?* (singular)

Repeat the procedure with the remaining phrases.

Name_____ Date_____

Form Possessives

> Use **possessives** when writing to show that a person, place, or thing has or owns something.
>
> • the books of the students = **the students' books**
> • the toys of the children = **the children's toys**

Rewrite the sentences using the correct possessive forms.

1. I carried the groceries that belong to Ms. Smith up the stairs.

_____

2. Daniel returned the shovel that belongs to his father to the garage.

_____

3. The boys washed the car that belongs to Mr. Hess.

_____

4. Jenna may ride the scooter that belongs to her sister in the park.

_____

5. The crowing of the roosters woke us up early.

_____

6. We were surprised by the cries of the children.

_____

Common Core
State Standard

L.3.2d

Name_____ Date_____

Form Possessives

Write the possessive form for the underlined phrases on the line.

1. The <u>books that belong to Rita</u> are on the table.

_____

2. The new treasurer will be the <u>choice of the people</u>.

_____

3. <u>The winner of today</u> is Mr. Wilson. _____

4. Marietta has asked for the <u>old skates of Julia</u>. _____

Write the correctly punctuated possessive form of the phrase in parentheses on the line.

5. I will clean my (father's garage, fathers' garage) on Saturday.

_____

6. Ms. Rogers has the (actors' costumes,

actor's costumes) for the show.

_____

7. Tita brushed (Maria's hair, Marias' hair) before school.

_____

8. Kim collected her (class' homework, class's homework).

_____

Common Core Language Grade 3 • ©2014 Newmark Learning, LLC

COMMON CORE
STATE STANDARD
L.3.2d

Name_____ Date_____

Use Possessives

Write a sentence using the possessive form of each phrase.

1. the ice cream of the boy

_____

2. the croaking of the frogs

_____

3. the notebook of Tomas

_____

4. the answer of the children

_____

5. the squeaking of the mice

_____

6. the whiskers of the cat

_____

7. the mittens of Lana

_____

8. the pencil of Ross

_____

COMMON CORE
STATE STANDARD
L.3.2e

Use Conventional Spelling

> **COMMON CORE STATE STANDARD L.3.2e**
> Use conventional spelling for high-frequency and other studied words and for adding suffixes to base words (e.g., *sitting, smiled, cries, happiness*).

Explain

Tell students that the spelling of some words should be memorized, especially words that we read and use often. Explain that there are rules to follow for adding suffixes to base words that can help them spell words correctly.

Say: *A suffix is word part added to the end of a word that changes the base word's meaning. For many words, the suffixes are added directly to the end of the base word. For other words, there are certain spelling rules to follow.*

Model

Write the following words on the board:

1. *cry, cried, crying*
2. *big, bigger, biggest*
3. *smile, smiled, smiling*
4. *happy, happier, happiest, happily*

Say: *Many words that end in -y, such as* cry, *have a rule for adding a suffix. The rule is change the -y to an -i. When adding the suffix -ed, change the -y to -i. But when adding -ing, don't change the -y to -i, just add the suffix.*

Say: *If we add suffixes to other words, we follow doubling rules. If a short word ends in a single consonant, like* sit, *double the last letter when adding a suffix. Sit becomes* sitting *with two t's. We follow the doubling rule for longer words that end in other consonants, such as -l, -n, and -m. For example,* swim *becomes* swimming *with two m's.*

Say: *If a word ends with a silent -e, there is another rule: drop the silent -e when adding a suffix. Smile becomes* smiled *or* smiling. *Learn when to follow these rules, and use a dictionary to be sure the words are spelled correctly.*

Guide Practice

Write these words on the board: *eat, cry, happy, hid, hopeful*. Ask students to come to the board and add appropriate suffixes to each word (*eating, cried, crying, happier, happiest, happily, hiding, hopefully*). Have students write these new words under the root words.

Name_____ Date_____

High-Frequency Words

High-frequency words are words that appear most often in books. They are sometimes called **sight words** because some of them can't be sounded out. They need to be learned by sight. It is important to memorize the spellings of these words.

Circle the word that is spelled correctly in each pair.

1. eight, eihgt

2. trie, try

3. abowt, about

4. lite, light

5. laugh, laff

6. myself, miself

7. realy, really

8. can't, cant

9. pleas, please

10. becuse, because

11. would, woud

12. tooday, today

13. these, theese

14. owen, own

15. together, toogether

16. clean, cleen

17. their, thier

18. ownly, only

19. wash, wach

20. right, ryght

Name_____ Date_____

High-Frequency Words

Circle any misspelled words in the following sentences. Then rewrite the sentence correctly.

1. Liam herd the sownd of the fountin in the gardin.

_____

_____

2. The third grade teecher cheked each student's homework.

_____

_____

3. Gary turnt off the lights to save energe.

_____

_____

4. Tomorow we will practis frakshons in school.

_____

_____

5. We folowed along as Ms. Farrel cheked our ansers.

_____

_____

Name_____ Date_____

Adding Suffixes

When adding a **suffix**, remember when to change a
-**y** to an -**i** or double a letter. For some words, a
dictionary may have to be used.

- beg   beg**ged**
- berry   berr**ies**

Write the following words with *-ed* and *-ing* suffixes.

1. prepare _____

_____

2. hug _____

_____

3. raise _____

_____

Write the following words with *-er*, *-est*, and *-ly* suffixes.

4. noisy _____

_____

5. grand _____

_____

6. close _____

_____

Name_____ Date_____

Adding Suffixes

Write the following words with *-ed* and *-ing* suffixes.

1. welcome _____

2. belong _____

3. flow _____

Write the following words with *-er* and *-est* suffixes.

4. big _____

5. hot _____

6. red _____

Write the following words with *-est* and *-ly* endings.

7. fierce _____

8. blind _____

9. fresh _____

Name_____ Date_____

Adding Suffixes

Read each sentence. Add a suffix to the underlined word so that it makes sense in the sentence and write the new word on the line.

1. Manuel <u>calm</u> read his book report in class. _____

2. Mother grew <u>tear</u> when she read the greeting card. _____

3. That kitten is <u>playful</u> chasing the ball. _____

4. Tomas likes to read the <u>late</u> adventure books. _____

5. Grandma is <u>collect</u> stamps from other countries. _____

6. Sylvia likes to splash in puddles on <u>rain</u> days. _____

7. Dad says the puppy must stop <u>beg</u> for treats. _____

8. Sara can jump <u>high</u> than her brother can. _____

9. The tiny baby chose the <u>big</u> teddy bear. _____

10. Yesterday at the zoo, Paul <u>laugh</u> at the penguins. _____

11. The birds have eaten the <u>juice</u> berries. _____

12. Mia's backpack feels <u>light</u> than mine. _____

COMMON CORE
STATE STANDARD
L.3.2f

Use Spelling Patterns and Generalizations

> **COMMON CORE STATE STANDARD L.3.2f**
> Use spelling patterns and generalizations (e.g., *word families, position-based spellings, syllable patterns, ending rules, meaningful word parts*) in writing words.

Explain
Tell students that some spelling patterns help us remember how to spell words.

Say: *Some words follow spelling patterns and rules for different sounds. We have learned to use word families, find syllable patterns, and know rules for adding word endings. Knowing these patterns helps you decode and spell many new words. Words don't always follow these rules and patterns, but knowing them helps. Let's review some of these spelling patterns.*

short vowels to long vowels
No final e to final e (kit, kite)
dge to ge (badge, cage)
tch to ch (catch, reach)

long vowel digraphs
ay, ai (play, wait)
ee, ea (feet, team)
ie, igh (tie, light)
oa, ow (boat, grow)

blends
bl, fl, sl (blot, flat, slip)
br, dr, tr (brim, drip, trap)
sm, sp, sw (small, spot, swim)
nd, lt, mp (land, felt, lamp)
spl, squ, str (split, squid, strap)

consonant digraphs
ck (deck); ch (chin); sh (shut)
th (that); wh (what)

r-controlled digraphs
ar (park)
ur/er/ir/ur (burn, clerk, bird, fur)
or/ore/oar (port, tore, roar)
eer/ear (steer, hear)
air/are (fair, dare)

variant vowels
oo/ue/ew (broom, blue, grew)
oo/ou (took, should)
aw/au/augh (draw, cause, caught)

diphthongs
ou/ow (found, plow)
oi/oy (boil, boy)

silent letters
kn/wr/mb (know, wrong, lamb)

Model
Write *kit* and *car* on the board. Ask for volunteers to pronounce these words. Add a final e to each (*kite, care*). Ask for volunteers to pronounce these words.

Ask: *How does the final e change the sound of the vowel? How does this help us know how to spell words?* (Many words with long vowels end in silent e.)

Review other patterns and rules from the chart.

Name_____ Date_____

COMMON CORE
STATE STANDARD
L.3.2f

Use Spelling Patterns and Generalizations

Use spelling patterns and rules to correct the spelling of underlined words.
Rewrite the sentence correctly on the line.

1. The <u>mon</u> <u>ros</u> in the <u>nit</u> sky. _____

_____

2. The <u>cacher</u> <u>cot</u> the <u>firs</u> <u>pich</u>. _____

_____

3. Lisa <u>liks</u> to <u>splas</u> in the <u>pul</u> on hot days. _____

_____

4. The <u>kit</u> <u>climed</u> <u>hier</u> as we raced <u>thru</u> the park. _____

_____

5. Laura <u>rapped</u> the <u>scaf</u> around her <u>nek</u>. _____

_____

6. The lion <u>yoned</u> in its <u>cag</u> and <u>likked</u> its <u>wiskers</u>. _____

_____

COMMON CORE
STATE STANDARD
L.3.2f

Name_____ Date_____

Use Spelling Patterns and Generalizations

Correct the spelling of the underlined words in each sentence. Write the sentence correctly on the line.

1. We <u>driv</u> <u>ner</u> the <u>libary</u> <u>wen</u> we visit <u>or</u> <u>Ant</u> Annie.

_____

2. <u>Ples</u> <u>rap</u> the <u>sandwices</u> in <u>foyl</u>.

_____

3. The <u>flite</u> was <u>lat</u> so Maria waited at the airport.

_____

4. I will give this <u>not</u> to your <u>tecer</u>.

_____

5. Tony <u>skwezed</u> the water out of the <u>sopy</u> <u>spongs</u>.

_____

6. The wind <u>rored</u> and <u>roked</u> the boat.

_____

7. Mimi steered her bicycle <u>arown</u> the obstacle <u>cors</u>.

_____

8. Nina's <u>favrit</u> color is <u>blu</u>.

_____

9. Dan fills his mug to the <u>bim</u> with warm milk every <u>nit</u>.

_____

10. We <u>nu</u> Brian <u>wud</u> <u>pla</u> baseball today.

_____

Name_____ Date_____

COMMON CORE
STATE STANDARD
L.3.2f

Use Spelling Patterns and Generalizations

Circle the correctly spelled word to complete each sentence.

1. Since the storm, the tree (leens, leans) to the left.

2. Grandpa (mite, might) visit us on New Year's Day.

3. Sun's water bottle fell and (landed, laded) on the stairs.

4. Ginny smoothed out the (rinkles, wrinkles) in her new dress.

5. Dad likes the clowns because they make him (laugh, laff).

Choose five correctly spelled words from the box.
Use each word to write a sentence.
Underline the word you use in the sentence.

taught	walk	badge	curage	freez	lean	flight
caught	com	div	clere	delishus	nock	wait

6. _____

_____

7. _____

_____

8. _____

_____

9. _____

_____

10. _____

_____

COMMON CORE
STATE STANDARD

L.3.2g

Use Reference Materials for Spelling

> **COMMON CORE STATE STANDARD L.3.2g**
> Consult reference materials, including beginning dictionaries, as needed to check and correct spellings.

Explain
Tell students how to use reference materials to look up the correct spellings.

Say: *When you do not know how to spell a word, you can use different types of reference materials such as glossaries, spellchecker on your computer, or an online or print version of a dictionary. When using a spellchecker or dictionary, it is important to make sure the word's definition matches the word we are using.*

Model
Show students an example of a dictionary page.

---

flounce
flounder
flour [flowr]
    (noun) finely ground, sifted grain used in baking
flourish
flow
flower [FLOW-er]
    (noun) a blossom that blooms on a plant
    (verb) to produce flowers
flu

Point out that all of these words are on one page of a print dictionary. **Say:** *Today we are focusing on the words* flour *and* flower. Explain that if you were writing a recipe, you might need to use the word *flour*. If you weren't sure how to spell it, you could make your best guess and look it up in a dictionary. Does it begin with *f-l-o-u* or *f-l-o-w*? To be sure, you can read the definitions of both words to determine that the word *f-l-o-u-r* is the correct meaning and spelling of the word you need for your recipe. Display an online dictionary.

Guide Practice
Have students work with partners and give each pair a dictionary. Tell them a word to look up and ask them the following questions:

1. Write the word. (glance)
2. What is one meaning of this word? (to take a quick look at)
3. Use the word in a sentence. (I glanced at my book.)

Repeat the procedure with other words.

Name_____ Date_____

COMMON CORE
STATE STANDARD
L.3.2g

Use Reference Materials for Spelling

We can use different types of **reference materials** to help us spell words, such as an online or print version of a dictionary. When using a **print version** of a dictionary, use guide words to find words quickly and easily. When using an **online version** of a dictionary, type your spelling tries into the search bar and check what pops up.

Use a print or digital dictionary or other reference to check the spelling of the words below. If the word is misspelled, provide the correct spelling.

1. buterfly _____

2. famus _____

3. cloud _____

4. curtin _____

5. sevendy _____

6. notice _____

7. honnor _____

8. written _____

9. receve _____

10. lonly _____

Common Core
State Standard

L.3.2g

Name_____ Date_____

Use Reference Materials for Spelling

Think of a word that fits each description and write it on the line. Look up the word in a print or digital dictionary or other reference materials.

1. A hot and dry land with few plants and little rainfall

_____

2. The hairy coat of an animal

_____

3. A baseball player who throws the ball

_____

4. a short sleep

_____

5. a place to go when sick or hurt for care

_____

Look up the word *radiant* in a print or digital dictionary. Use *radiant* in a sentence.

_____

_____

_____

_____

Name_____ Date_____

COMMON CORE
STATE STANDARD
L.3.2g

Use Reference Materials for Spelling

Tell whether each word would be found on the dictionary page with the guide words *pale* and *pine*. Write *yes* or *no*.

1. plane _____

2. peddler _____

3. parent _____

4. pack _____

5. paid _____

6. pencil _____

7. pour _____

8. president _____

9. pilot _____

10. piano _____

Check the spelling of each word using reference materials. If the word is spelled correctly, write *correct*. If it is not, write the correct spelling.

11. recieved _____

12. intresting _____

13. diffrent _____

14. beleive _____

15. really _____

16. allways _____

COMMON CORE
STATE STANDARD

L.3.3a

Choose Words and Phrases for Effect

> **COMMON CORE STATE STANDARD L.3.3a**
> Choose words and phrases for effect.

Explain
Tell students that they can choose words that make a picture in the listener's or reader's mind.

Say: *When you choose words or phrases for effect, they help people understand exactly what you mean.*

Model
On the board, write two sentences:

1. *A child went over a wall.*
2. *A small, dark-haired girl in a red shirt scrambled over the high stone wall.*

Say: *Which sentence gives you a better picture in your mind? The descriptive words in the second sentence tell you much more about the scene. You all probably have a similar picture in your minds. Descriptive words are usually adjectives and adverbs, but verbs and nouns can be descriptive, too.*

Ask for volunteers to circle the descriptive words. If they don't circle the verb *scrambled* or the noun *girl*, ask them to compare the second sentence to the first sentence.

Say: *What details do the verb* scramble *and the noun* girl *add? They are descriptive, too. There is a big difference between the verbs* went *or* ran *or* climbed *and the verb* scrambled, *as well as the nouns* child *or* person *and the noun* girl.

Guide Practice
On the board, write four headings—*Adjectives, Adverbs, Nouns,* and *Verbs*. Write the following descriptive words under the appropriate heading. Then ask the students to add to the lists.

Say: *These words are used for effect, to help you be clear about what you want to say. What are some other descriptive words that we can add to these lists?*

Adjectives	Adverbs	Nouns	Verbs
light blue	quietly	ant	amaze
itchy	politely	expert	wander
steep	lazily	recliner	exclaim

Name_____ Date_____

COMMON CORE
STATE STANDARD
L.3.3a

Choose Words and Phrases for Effect

> Using **descriptive language** means choosing words and phrases for effect. The words should give the reader or listener a clear picture.
>
> - The boy went for a walk.
> - The **young** boy **decided** to take a **long stroll through the beautiful park**.

Circle the descriptive words in the following story.

It was a bright afternoon in early September when Drummer came to the farm. Hardly more than a colt, he dashed across the lush pasture and into the shade of the sugar maples. It was there that he first saw Elizabeth, who had been wishing for him for five long years. He trotted over to the fence and watched as she unfolded her legs and stood up staring as though she could hardly believe he was real. A squeal escaped from her lips, and she rushed toward him and leaped onto the fence. He bolted. Her sudden charge had spooked him, and he ran two wide circles around the field before his curiosity forced him back to her side of the fence. They stood gazing at each other again until Elizabeth slowly put out her hand. Drummer moved toward her and she gently stroked the horse's velvety nose.

Write a new, more descriptive word for each of the following words.

1. thin _____

2. very _____

3. dog _____

4. walk _____

COMMON CORE
STATE STANDARD

L.3.3a

Name_____ Date_____

Choose Words and Phrases for Effect

**Use adjectives to make these sentences more descriptive.
Use more than one adjective for a noun if needed.**

1. The _____ cat slept on the _____ chair in the _____ room.

2. My _____ Aunt Daria loves her _____ car, which is _____ and _____.

3. Don't forget the _____ bag when you take the _____ bus to the _____ store.

4. Little Ina's _____ hair was the hit of the _____ parade in the _____ town of Brookdale.

5. The _____ field was speckled with _____ flowers and _____ birds.

Add an adverb to each sentence to make it more descriptive.

6. The team _____ played its way to a close victory.

7. After the argument, Ezra walked _____ away.

8. Karly stood up and _____ recited her poem.

9. Arturo climbed the stairs _____ and went to bed.

10. We danced _____ past my sister's room on our way to the kitchen.

Name_____ Date_____

COMMON CORE
STATE STANDARD
L.3.3a

Choose Words and Phrases for Effect

Use descriptive language to rewrite the sentences below.

1. A man went to a store.

_____

2. A child caught a bug.

_____

3. A girl sang a song.

_____

4. Someone sat on a chair.

_____

5. She went home.

_____

6. A boy rode in a car.

_____

Write a short paragraph using descriptive language about what happens on the first day of school.

_____

_____

_____

_____

_____

COMMON CORE
STATE STANDARD

L.3.3b

Differences Between Spoken and Written Language

> **COMMON CORE STATE STANDARD L.3.3b**
> Recognize and observe differences between the conventions of spoken and written standard English.

Explain
Written and spoken language may have different purposes and may follow different guidelines.

Say: *The way we speak is not the way we write. We follow many rules when writing to make sure words are spelled correctly, the sentences are formed correctly, and meaning is clear. This is standard English. We use standard English when writing a report, doing homework, and writing a letter.*

Model
Write the following sentences on the board:

1. *Because there were so many people waiting, we decided to leave and return at a later time.*

2. *There were tons of people in line, so we got out of there and came back later.*

Read each sentence aloud, pointing to the words as you speak. Point out that the first sentence follows conventions of grammar and spelling, or standard English. The second sentence more closely follows English as it may be spoken in conversation.

Guide Practice
Write these words and expressions on the board: *hang out, awesome, knock it off, buddy.*

Ask a volunteer if he or she can think of a standard English sentence using the first expression. Have the student write the sentence on the board. (Sample response: *The flag will hang out of the window.*)

Ask: *Is this expression a good fit for formal writing? How often do you think you would use it in a report or other assignment?*

Have the students offer examples of everyday language in which they might use the expression. (Sample response: *Dan and I will hang out at the playground.*) Point out the differences in formal and informal uses. Repeat the process with the remaining words and expressions.

Name_____ Date_____

COMMON CORE
STATE STANDARD
L.3.3b

Recognize and Observe Differences Between Spoken and Written Language

Read the following passage. Rewrite it using standard English.

I read this awesome book about this cat—she's named Milly—who solves this mystery. Someone's stealing packages. Milly's owner, he's really kinda her friend, is a mail carrier named Harley. She follows him all over town. She asks a bunch of cats and stuff, like mice, who's been stealing the boxes. Milly puts clues where Harley can't miss them, so he thinks he's some kind of detective for figuring it all out. But he isn't. 'Cause Milly did all the work. But it's okay 'cause in the book she really likes him a lot and the adventures are real fun.

_____

_____

_____

_____

_____

_____

_____

COMMON CORE
STATE STANDARD

L.3.3b

Name_____ Date_____

Recognize and Observe Differences Between Spoken and Written Language

Read the following letter. Rewrite it using standard English.

Hey Uncle Martin!

Camping has been really cool. I'm glad you gave us the idea to give it a go. Yesterday, first thing, we went on a hike. We walked through these pine trees and we saw about a million birds.

We hang around the campfire at night, eating dinner, talking, looking at the sky and stuff like that. Next on our list: Rowing. Mom says she'll show me the ropes.

Thanks for letting us borrow your tent, it's awesome having my own room! See ya next week.

Later,

Taylor

_____

_____

_____

_____

_____

_____

_____

_____

Name_____ Date_____

COMMON CORE
STATE STANDARD
L.3.3b

Recognize and Observe Differences Between Spoken and Written Language

Read the following sentences. Rewrite them using standard English.

1. Molly, eatin' a sandwich, wrote up her book report.

_____

2. Dan headed to the library to take his books back.

_____

3. Lina's little sis hams it up when her daddy takes pics.

_____

4. Hit the lights!

_____

5. We met indoors. Because of all the rain.

_____

6. His sister. The older one. She can bring us home later.

_____

7. Dina headed to the new park to check it out.

_____

8. Harry's bro's crazy over the kittens.

_____

COMMON CORE
STATE STANDARD

L.3.3b

Name_____ Date_____

Recognize and Observe Differences Between Spoken and Written Language

Think of a recent conversation you've had with a friend, teacher, or family member. For example, maybe you talked about a television show, video game, or sporting event. Write a passage about the discussion using standard English.

_____

_____

_____

_____

_____

_____

_____

_____

_____

_____

Lesson Plan Teacher Worksheet
Vocabulary Acquisition and Use

The lessons in this section are organized in the same order as the Common Core Language Standards for vocabulary acquisition and use. Each mini-lesson provides specific, explicit instruction for a Language standard and is followed by multiple practice pages. Use the following chart to track the standards students have practiced. You may wish to revisit mini-lessons and practice pages a second time for spiral review.

Common Core State Standard	Mini-Lessons and Practice	Page	Complete (✓)	Review (✓)
L.3.4a	Mini-Lesson 23: Use Sentence-Level Context	118		
	Practice Pages: Use Sentence-Level Context	119		
L.3.4b	Mini-Lesson 24: Affixes: Prefixes and Suffixes	122		
	Practice Pages: Affixes: Prefixes and Suffixes	123		
L.3.4c	Mini-Lesson 25: Root Words	128		
	Practice Pages: Root Words	129		
L.3.4d	Mini-Lesson 26: Use Glossaries or Dictionaries to Determine Meaning	132		
	Practice Pages: Use Glossaries or Dictionaries to Determine Meaning	133		
L.3.5a	Mini-Lesson 27: Distinguish Literal and Nonliteral Meanings	136		
	Practice Pages: Distinguish Literal and Nonliteral Meanings	137		
L.3.5b	Mini-Lesson 28: Identify Real-Life Connections	140		
	Practice Pages: Identify Real-Life Connections	141		
L.3.5c	Mini-Lesson 29: Shades of Meaning	144		
	Practice Pages: Shades of Meaning	145		
	Answer Key	166		

COMMON CORE
STATE STANDARD
L.3.4a

Use Sentence-Level Context

> **COMMON CORE STATE STANDARD L.3.4a**
> Use sentence-level context as a clue to the meaning of a word or phrase.

Explain

Tell students how to use context clues to determine the meaning of words.

Say: *When we read, we use context clues to help us figure out the meaning of new words. As writers, we can include context clues for our readers, too. We can use information from a dictionary or thesaurus as well as what we already know about words. A context clue can be a definition, description, example, synonym, or antonym.*

Model

Write these sentences on the board:

1. *My grandma makes the best custard, which is a sweet, pudding-like dessert made with milk and eggs.* (definition)
2. *Serena helped her mom make smooth, creamy custard for dessert.* (description)
3. *I like to eat desserts like custard, pudding, and mousse.* (example)
4. *I ordered the custard, or pudding, from the dessert list.* (synonym)
5. *Dad likes custard better than cake because it is creamier than cake.* (antonym)

Discuss each example, pointing out how the words and phrases give more information about the meaning of the word *custard* and help readers visualize what *custard* is, what it looks like, and what it tastes like. From the context clues in the sentences, students can determine that *custard* is a smooth dessert that tastes sweet and creamy and is like pudding.

Guide Practice

Write the following sentences on the board. Ask a volunteer to circle the context clue(s) for the word *cardigan* in the first sentence.

1. *Mr. Rogers liked to wear a type of button-front sweater called a cardigan.* (type of button-front sweater)
2. *He turned on the lantern so he could see because it was dark.* (see, dark)

Repeat the procedure. Have the students find the context clues for lantern in the second sentence. Remind them that context clues help us figure out the meanings of words that we may not know.

Name_____ Date_____

COMMON CORE
STATE STANDARD

L.3.4a

Use Sentence-Level Context

Context clues help us figure out the meaning of new words. A **context clue** can be a definition, description, example, synonym, or antonym.

- The paper felt <u>stiff</u> **like a board**.
- She wrapped a <u>scarf</u> **around her neck to stay warm**.

Use context clues to determine the meaning of the underlined word. Write the definition of the word on the line.

1. The plumber <u>repaired</u> the leaky sink, and it no longer drips water.

   _____

2. The old woman <u>moaned</u> quietly to herself as she lifted the heavy bag with her sore arm.

   _____

3. Because I wasn't paying attention, I was <u>stumped</u> when the teacher asked me the correct answer.

   _____

4. The rowboat <u>drifted</u> slowly down the stream.

   _____

5. The sad movie made her <u>weep</u>, and tears dripped down her face.

   _____

COMMON CORE
STATE STANDARD

L.3.4a

Name_____ Date_____

Use Sentence-Level Context

Use context clues to figure out the meaning of the underlined word. Circle the correct meaning of the underlined word.

1. Tommy strummed the strings of the <u>banjo</u> to play music.

   Ⓐ instrument

   Ⓑ plant

   Ⓒ book

2. The <u>hue</u> of the sky matched her big blue eyes.

   Ⓐ cloud

   Ⓑ color

   Ⓒ sound

3. A desert is an <u>arid</u> land that has little water.

   Ⓐ dry

   Ⓑ cool

   Ⓒ loud

4. Barkly did like to wear <u>trousers</u> as much as he liked to wear shorts and jeans.

   Ⓐ shirts

   Ⓑ pants

   Ⓒ socks

5. Mom told me to <u>remain</u> in one place if I ever get separated from her.

   Ⓐ stay

   Ⓑ move

   Ⓒ look

Name_____ Date_____

COMMON CORE
STATE STANDARD
L.3.4a

Use Sentence-Level Context

**Complete the sentences below using words from the box.
Use context clues from the sentences to choose the correct word.**

brilliant	delicate	irate
kneaded	pleasant	starving

1. Rodney didn't have time to eat breakfast, so he was

_____ by lunch time.

2. The store clerk told Cindy not to touch the glass flower

because it was _____.

3. My older sister is usually crabby, but today she seemed

_____.

4. The baker turned, rubbed, and _____ the dough

into a smooth ball.

5. The sunset looked _____ against the dark sky.

6. My dad was _____ because I missed the bus,

and he had to come get me.

Write a sentence for the word *nibble* using context clues.

_____

_____

_____

COMMON CORE
STATE STANDARD
L.3.4b

Affixes: Prefixes and Suffixes

> **COMMON CORE STATE STANDARD L.3.4b**
>
> Determine the meaning of the new word formed when a known affix is added to a known word (e.g., *agreeable/disagreeable, comfortable/ uncomfortable, care/careless, heat/preheat*).

Explain

Tell students that a prefix comes at the beginning of a root word and a suffix comes at the end of a root word. They change the word's meaning.

Say: *When you know the meanings of prefixes and suffixes, you can use them to figure out the meanings of new words. When you are reading and you come across a word you don't know, use context clues to figure out its meaning. Context clues are words in the sentence that help you understand what the new word means.*

Model

Write *healthy* and *unhealthy* on the board, and underline the prefix *un-*.

Say: *You can see that* unhealthy *is the word* healthy *with the prefix* un- *at the beginning. The prefix* un- *means "not," so it changes the meaning to "not healthy."* Then display the following prefix chart.

Prefix	Meaning	Example
un-	not, opposite of	unhealthy
re-	again, back	rewrap
mis-	wrong or wrongly	misjudge
pre-	before	precook

Guide Practice

Write the following words on the board: *reheat, uncurl, misspeak, precut.* Have volunteers circle the prefix in each word, tell what the prefix means, and then use the prefix and the root word to figure out the word's meaning. Then add each word to the chart. Repeat the procedure using suffixes.

Suffix	Meaning	Example
-ful	full of	healthful
-less	without	fearless
-er	more	harder
-est	most	weakest

COMMON CORE
STATE STANDARD
L.3.4b

Name_____ Date_____

Prefixes

A **prefix** is a group of letters at the beginning of a word that change the word's meaning.

- **un**- not   unhappy (not happy)
- **re**- again   retell (tell again)
- **mis**- wrong   misspell (spell wrong)
- **pre**- before   preschool (before school)

Underline the prefix in the following words. Write the meaning of the word on the line.

1. unsafe _____

2. rebuild _____

3. mistreat _____

4. precook _____

5. unable _____

6. unstick _____

7. rethink _____

8. refill _____

9. misspell _____

10. misplace _____

COMMON CORE
STATE STANDARD
L.3.4b

Name_____ Date_____

Prefixes

Choose the correct prefix from the box to make the word match the definition in parentheses.

un-	re-	mis-	pre-

1. _____ dawn   (before dawn)

2. _____ fasten   (fasten again)

3. _____ packaged   (packaged before)

4. _____ use   (use again)

5. _____ behave   (behave wrongly)

6. _____ healthy   (not healthy)

7. _____ lead   (lead wrongly)

8. _____ painted   (not painted)

Read each sentence. Write the correct word from the box on the line.

preschool	refill	unfair	misunderstood	uneven

9. I tripped because the sidewalk was _____.

10. I got the homework wrong because I _____ the directions.

11. My glass was empty so I asked my dad to _____ it.

12. My sister thinks it is _____ that I get to stay up as late as she does.

13. Mike's younger brother goes to the same _____ as my little sister.

Name_____ Date_____

Suffixes

A **suffix** is a group of letters at the end of a word that change the word's meaning.

- **-ful**   full of   hopeful (full of hope)
- **-less**   without   hopeless (without hope)
- **-er**   more   stronger (more strong)
- **-est**   most   strongest (most strong)

Underline the suffix in each sentence. Then write the definition of the word on the line.

1. Kara is a lot taller than Reilly. _____

2. We had a wonderful time at the park. _____

3. My father is the smartest man I know. _____

4. The flowers in Grammy's garden are beautiful. _____

5. That was the loudest music he had ever heard. _____

6. Ricardo is fearless when he races his bicycle. _____

Combine each word with the suffix to make a new word.

7. boast + ful = _____   **11.** bold + er = _____

8. dark + est = _____   **12.** wild + est = _____

9. cold + er = _____   **13.** faith + ful = _____

10. help + less = _____   **14.** care + less = _____

COMMON CORE
STATE STANDARD
L.3.4b

Name_____ Date_____

Suffixes

Write a definition for the underlined word on the line.

1. In winter the world seems <u>colorless</u>.

_____

2. Jason was <u>careful</u> not to cut himself on the broken glass.

_____

3. It was the <u>highest</u> hill we had ever climbed.

_____

4. Our teacher is always <u>truthful</u> with us.

_____

5. Jenna scrubbed the toys until they were <u>spotless</u>.

_____

6. That huge truck is almost <u>wider</u> than the road.

_____

Add a suffix to each word. Then write a sentence using the word.

7. help _____

_____

_____

8. harm _____

_____

_____

9. play _____

_____

_____

Common Core Language Grade 3 • ©2014 Newmark Learning, LLC

Name_____ Date_____

Prefixes and Suffixes

Fill in the blank using a word with a prefix or suffix that matches the definition in parentheses.

1. Greg went _____ to the beach and ended up with a sunburn. (without a shirt)

2. Alex loves the _____ leaves in the fall. (full of color)

3. Rita thought it was _____ that Cody went to the movies. (not fair)

4. My dog Flip always _____ when we have company. (behaves badly)

5. Martin tried to be _____ when his grandfather worked in the yard. (full of help)

6. Being smaller than everyone else makes my youngest cousin feel _____. (without power)

7. The new uniforms cost so much, we decided to _____ the old ones. (use again)

8. The new doghouse was finished except for being _____. (not painted)

9. Our class took a _____ to practice our spelling. (before test)

10. Ms. Thompson said I had to _____ my homework. (do again)

COMMON CORE
STATE STANDARD

L.3.4c

Root Words

> **COMMON CORE STATE STANDARD L.3.4c**
> Use a known root word as a clue to the meaning of an unknown word with the same root (e.g., *company, companion*).

Explain

Tell students that larger words can be formed from basic words called root words.

Say: *Root words will help you figure out the meanings of words that come from the same root.*

Model

On the board, write *truth* and *truthful* and underline the root word *truth* in each word.

Say: *You can see that the word* truthful *is the root word* truth *with the ending* -ful. *You can use the meaning of* truth *(honesty) to figure out the meaning of* truthful. *The word* truthful *means "full of truth" or "very honest."*

Show the students this chart.

Word	Root + Ending	Meaning
truthful	truth + -ful	full of truth, honest
worthless	worth + -less	without worth
brightest	bright + -est	most bright

Say: *In this chart, you can see words that combine roots and common endings.*

Point out the word *truthful* in the first row of the chart. Point to the word *worthless* and ask students to identify the root word (worth) and underline it.

Say: *Suppose I read the word* worthless, *but I'm not sure what it means. I can see that the word is formed from the root word* worth *and the ending* -less: worth *+* –less *=* worthless. *I know that the word* worth *means "value or price" and that the ending* -less *means "without." Now I can figure out that* worthless *means "without value."*

Follow a similar procedure to discuss the remaining examples in the chart.

Guide Practice

On the board, write the following words for practice: *wasteful, helpless, freshest.* Ask for volunteers to underline the root word in each word. Then use the root word and ending to figure out the word's meaning. Add each word to the chart.

COMMON CORE
STATE STANDARD
L.3.4c

Name_____ Date_____

Root Words

> Remember that a **root word** has no prefixes or suffixes. A prefix is a word part that comes before a root word. A suffix is a word part that comes after.
>
> | Prefix | Suffix |
> |--------|--------|
> | <u>re</u>think | thought<u>ful</u> |
> | <u>un</u>tie | strong<u>est</u> |

Write the root of each word on the line.

1. rehang _____

2. forgetful _____

3. thoughtless _____

4. misbehave _____

5. weakest _____

6. unbutton _____

7. biggest _____

8. wishful _____

9. preheat _____

10. beautiful _____

COMMON CORE
STATE STANDARD
L.3.4c

Name_____ Date_____

Root Words

Write a definition for each underlined word in each sentence.

1. Henry thought it was <u>useless</u> to beg his parents for a puppy.

_____

2. I didn't think the plant was <u>harmful</u>, but it gave me a rash.

_____

3. Since the coat was <u>unworn</u>, Hazel returned it to the store.

_____

4. The old cat was <u>livelier</u> than usual, jumping from chair to chair.

_____

5. Jen's <u>mistrust</u> made her walk away without buying the ring.

_____

6. Dad sliced the meat into the <u>thinnest</u> pieces.

_____

7. I was so hungry, I ate a big <u>plateful</u> of pasta.

_____

8. Mom asked Kate to <u>preheat</u> the oven for dinner.

_____

Name_____ Date_____

Root Words

Add a prefix from the box to each root word, using each one only once. Then write a sentence using that word.

re	pre	un	mis

1. _____ + happy = _____

_____

2. _____ + guide = _____

_____

3. _____ + pack _____

_____

4. _____ + cook = _____

_____

Add a suffix from the box to each root word, using each one only once. Then write a sentence using that word.

er	est	ful	less

5. care + _____ = _____

_____

6. strange + _____ = _____

_____

7. smart + _____ = _____

_____

8. peace + _____ = _____

_____

COMMON CORE
STATE STANDARD

L.3.4d

Use Glossaries or Dictionaries to Determine Meaning

> **COMMON CORE STATE STANDARD L.3.4d**
> Use glossaries or beginning dictionaries, both print and digital, to determine or clarify the precise meaning of key words and phrases.

Explain

Tell students how to use glossaries or dictionaries to determine the meaning of words.

Say: *Sometimes when we write, we're not sure of a word's meaning. We may know the word but not its meaning. When this happens, we can use a glossary or dictionary to look up the meanings of words we don't know. Glossaries are alphabetical lists found at the end of books and contain meanings of certain words from that book. Dictionaries appear either in print or online and contain alphabetical lists of words.*

Model

Show students an example of a glossary or a dictionary page.

---

gath • er

(verb) to come together around a central point; assemble

(verb) to pick, collect, or accumulate

Say: *Imagine you are writing a story about flowers and you want to use the word* gather *to describe the act of picking the flowers. You are not sure that* gather *means what you think it does, so you need to look it up in a dictionary or glossary. After you look it up, you know that* gather *means* to pick *or* to collect. *Now you can use this word in your story.*

Then display an online dictionary and demonstrate how to type the word *gather* into the search bar.

Guide Practice

Pair up students and give each pair a dictionary. Tell them to look up the word *pitcher* and ask them the following questions:

1. Write the word. (*pitcher*)
2. What is one meaning of this word? (*a container for holding and pouring liquids*)
3. What is another meaning of this word? (*a baseball player who throws the ball*)
4. Use the word in a sentence using one meaning. (*I filled the pitcher with water.*)
5. Use the word in a sentence using another meaning. (*The pitcher struck out the batter.*)

Repeat the procedure with other words. Have the students go through the same procedure. Remind them to read the different meanings of a word, so they can use it correctly in a sentence.

Name_____ Date_____

COMMON CORE
STATE STANDARD
L.3.4d

Use Glossaries or Dictionaries to Determine Meaning

> If we are not sure of a word's meaning, we can use a **glossary** or a **dictionary** to look up the meaning of a word. Glossaries are found at the end of books and dictionaries appear either in print or online.

Use the glossary below to answer the questions.

Glossary of Weather Terms

Breeze: light wind

Lightning: a bright flash seen during a storm

Rain: water that falls from the sky

Snow: frozen water that falls from the sky in the winter

Thunder: the loud clap heard during a storm

---

1. What is not produced by a storm in the summer?

_____

2. What is heard during a storm?

_____

3. What is a bright flash seen during a storm?

_____

4. What is water called that falls from the sky?

_____

Common Core State Standard

L.3.4d

Name_____ Date_____

Use Glossaries or Dictionaries to Determine Meaning

Use a print or online dictionary to find the meaning of each word.

1. pilot

_____

_____

2. herd

_____

_____

3. divide

_____

_____

4. blossom

_____

_____

5. route

_____

_____

6. feast

_____

_____

COMMON CORE
STATE STANDARD
L.3.4d

Name_____ Date_____

Use Glossaries or Dictionaries to Determine Meaning

Use a print or online dictionary to find the meaning of each word. Then draw a line to match the word to its correct meaning.

1. eagle

a. an orange root vegetable

2. absorb

b. a large bird

3. ocean

c. a leader of a company or country

4. carrot

d. an army vehicle

5. tank

e. easily broken or damaged

6. ancient

f. to soak up or take in

7. nursery

g. traveling from one place to another

8. president

h. a large body of water

9. delicate

i. a place that grows young plants

10. journey

j. very old

COMMON CORE
STATE STANDARD

L.3.5a

Distinguish Literal and Nonliteral Meanings

> **COMMON CORE STATE STANDARD L.3.5a**
>
> Distinguish the literal and nonliteral meanings of words and phrases in context (e.g., *take steps*).

Explain

Tell students sometimes we don't mean the exact meaning of words. We need to study the context to know the meaning.

Say: *A literal meaning is exact. If you're on a baseball field and the coach tells you to* touch base, *you know exactly what to do. If you're here in class and I tell you to* touch base *with your partner on a group homework assignment, do I want you to go out to the baseball field? No! I want you to check with your partner to see if you're both making progress on the project.*

Explain

The phrase *touch base* has both a literal and a nonliteral meaning. Use context clues in the sentence to figure out which meaning the speaker or writer is using.

Model

Write the following sentences on the board.

1. *Take two <u>steps</u> forward.*
2. *We need to take <u>steps</u> to prepare for the test.*

Point out the underlined words in each sentence. Then point out the context in the first sentence, which tells how many and where. Point out the second sentence, in which the meaning is nonliteral. Tell the students the nonliteral use of the expression means to take action, but not walk steps.

Guide Practice

Write the following expressions on the board: *hang in there, lighten up, check it out, scoop.*

Ask a volunteer to write a sentence on the board using the first expression. (*I was worried about the math test but Dad said to hang in there and study.*)

Ask: *How do we know if the expression is meant literally or nonliterally? What are the clues to the meaning of the expression?*

Have students write their own sentences using the expressions and words. For each, ask them to try to write a sentence using the words literally and another using the words nonliterally.

136

Name_____ Date_____

COMMON CORE
STATE STANDARD
L.3.5a

Distinguish Literal and Nonliteral Meanings of Words/Phrases

**Read each sentence. Look at the underlined phrases.
Write whether the phrase is *literal* or *nonliteral* on the line.
Circle the context clues used.**

1. Grandpa's spaghetti sauce is <u>hands down</u> the best I've ever tasted.

_____

2. She put her <u>hands down</u> by her sides and stood in line.

_____

3. Martha climbed <u>on the fence</u> to watch the parade.

_____

4. Denny was <u>on the fence</u> about going to the dance.

_____

5. Jim was <u>in hot water</u> with the coach for missing practice.

_____

6. Kim put the carrots <u>in hot water</u> to cook them.

_____

7. Beth didn't want to cause trouble by <u>rocking the boat</u>.

_____

8. Lucy was <u>rocking the boat</u> on the water by running around.

_____

COMMON CORE
STATE STANDARD

L.3.5a

Name_____ Date_____

Distinguish Literal and Nonliteral Meanings of Words/Phrases

Read each sentence. Look at the underlined phrases. Write whether the phrase is *literal* or *nonliteral* on the line.

1. _____ The bulldozer covered trash down <u>in the dumps</u>.

2. _____ Tina was <u>down in the dumps</u> when her best friend changed schools.

3. _____ Mr. Turner <u>drew a blank</u> space on the board.

4. _____ Mary <u>drew a blank</u> when the teacher asked her to name the state capital.

5. _____ We expect <u>smooth sailing</u> at the soccer tournament.

6. _____ Captain Smith was blessed with <u>smooth sailing</u> on the Atlantic Ocean.

7. _____ The committee planned funding cuts <u>across the board</u>.

8. _____ One by one, we walked <u>across the board</u> to the other side of the creek.

9. _____ The detective thought the woman's story sounded <u>fishy</u>.

10. _____ Cooking crab cakes makes the house smell <u>fishy</u>.

Name_____ Date_____

COMMON CORE
STATE STANDARD
L.3.5a

Distinguish Literal and Nonliteral Meanings of Words/Phrases

Read the following sentences. Circle the words or phrases used nonliterally.

1. Will you please give me a hand with these groceries?

2. When Liam lagged behind in the store, his mother told him to step on it.

3. Susan and Mia drew a blank on the question so they put their hands down.

4. Greg lent a hand to Leo as they painted a mural on the fence.

5. Timmy is still down in the dumps over not being chosen for the team.

6. Rita, who has borrowed Mom's dress, will be in hot water if she steps on it.

Write two sentences using the following phrase: *knock it off*. Use it literally in the first sentence and nonliterally in the second sentence.

Literal

_____

_____

Nonliteral

_____

_____

COMMON CORE
STATE STANDARD
L.3.5b

Identify Real-Life Connections

> **COMMON CORE STATE STANDARD L.3.5.b**
> Identify real-life connections between words and their use (e.g., describe people who are *friendly* or *helpful*).

Explain

Tell students how to use real-life connections to understand the meaning of words.

Say: *Writers use what they know from their everyday lives in their writing. For example, you could easily make a list of people you would describe as friendly or helpful. Making and using these real-life connections between words helps us write more accurately and with greater detail.*

Model

Write the word *loud* on the board and ask the students to name some examples of real-life connections to the word. (examples: *yelling, screaming, children, concerts, fire trucks, airplanes, storms*)

Point out that many words come to mind when you say the word *loud*.

Say: *Fire trucks and airplanes are loud. Yelling and screaming is loud. Children and concerts can also be loud. Using real-life connections helps us write better.*

Guide Practice

Write these words on the board. Ask a volunteer to write at least one example of a real-life connection to the word in the first sentence. Then use both words in a sentence.

1. *cute* (puppy; The baby bird is cute, but not as cute as the puppy.)
2. *vast* (ocean; The ocean is vast.)
3. *hissed* (cat; The cat hissed as I walked by it.)

Ask: *Were you able to think of at least one word with a real-life connection to the word on the board and then write a sentence using both words?*

Repeat the procedure with each word. Have the students come up with at least one example of a real-life connection to each word and then use the words in a sentence.

Name_____ Date_____

COMMON CORE
STATE STANDARD
L.3.5b

Identify Real-Life Connections

> Writers use **real-life connections** to help readers better understand the meaning of words. Look at the words below. They are each followed by **real-life connections**. Think about how to use these connections to write interesting and descriptive sentences.
>
> - **red:** apples, tomatoes, raspberries, cherries, roses
> - **famous:** presidents, astronauts, athletes, movie stars, singers

Make a list of words with real-life connections to each word. Then write a sentence using the word and at least one connection.

1. safe, _____, _____, _____,

_____

_____

_____

2. fresh, _____, _____, _____,

_____

_____

_____

COMMON CORE
STATE STANDARD
L.3.5b

Name_____ Date_____

Identify Real-Life Connections Between Words and Their Use

Circle the word or words that make a real-life connection to the underlined word in each sentence.

1. The teacher used <u>simple</u> terms to explain the lesson, which made it easy to understand.

2. The <u>dull</u> story made him sleepy and distracted.

3. The sign was <u>round</u> like a ball or Earth.

4. The doctor told Eileen not to eat any <u>solid</u> foods and to eat soup, milkshakes, or applesauce instead.

5. Nancy didn't know why her hands were <u>sticky</u> since she didn't touch any gum, candy, or honey.

6. Patrick thought the joke that Pell told him was <u>hilarious</u>, and he laughed very loudly.

7. Jin's face got red and hot, and she felt <u>embarrassed</u> when she dropped her books in front of the group of students.

8. The hummingbird was <u>petite</u> just like a butterfly or daisy.

142

Name_____ Date_____

COMMON CORE
STATE STANDARD
L.3.5b

Identify Real-Life Connections Between Words and Their Use

Read the following passage and find the word *clumsy*. Share three real-life connections to the word *clumsy* from the story.

As Jeremiah trotted down the stairs, he lost one of his shoes and slipped down the rest of the steps. He got up, and as he brushed himself off, his elbow hit a picture frame. The frame fell to the ground, and it shattered into pieces. Jeremiah felt *clumsy*. He then grabbed a broom to clean up the mess.

_____

_____

_____

Think of at least one real-life connection to the word *clumsy* and write a sentence using the word *clumsy* and the real-life connection.

_____

_____

_____

_____

COMMON CORE
STATE STANDARD

L.3.5c

Shades of Meaning

> **COMMON CORE STATE STANDARD L.3.5c**
> Distinguish shades of meaning among related words that describe states of mind or degrees of certainty (e.g., *knew, believed, suspected, heard, wondered*).

Explain
Tell students that shades of meaning are the small differences between words that are related. Both verbs and adjectives can have shades of meaning.

Say: *Two words might have similar meanings, but one of the words may have a stronger meaning. Think about the words* mad *and* furious. *The word* furious *has a more powerful meaning than* mad.

Explain that knowing shades of meaning of verbs and adjectives can help make their writing and speaking not only more exact, but also more interesting.

Model
Write these groups of words on the board:

1. *nibble, chew, bite*
2. *big, huge, enormous*
3. *call, shout, yell*

Say: *Some of these words are stronger even though they all mean mostly the same thing. Nibble* is weaker than *bite, even though they both mean the same thing. Big* is weaker than *huge and* call *is weaker than* yell. *How you use the words depends on what you mean. You would use the word* nibble *to describe the way a mouse eats little pieces of cheese, but you would use the word* bite *to describe how a horse eats an apple.*

Guide Practice
Write these words on the board. Ask a volunteer to write at least one related word with a similar shade of meaning to the word in the first sentence.

1. *phony* (fake, pretend)
2. *embarrassed* (ashamed, mortified)
3. *cold* (frigid, freezing)

Ask: *Were you able to think of at least one word with the same shade of meaning?*

Repeat the procedure with each word.

Name_____ Date_____

Shades of Meaning

Many words mean almost the same thing but create different pictures. Writers must choose the right adjective or verb to best express what they mean.

Shades of Meaning for
States of Mind
- furious
- irate
- grumpy
- cross
- irritated

Shades of Meaning for
Degrees of Certainty
- knew
- believed
- suspected
- heard
- wondered

Circle the word in parentheses to complete the sentence.

1. He used the hammer to (tap, pound) the nails into the wood.

2. Margie (boasted, roared) to her friends about her good grades.

3. The librarian (murmured, snapped) at the children to be quiet.

4. Brian raised his hand confidently because he (knew, wondered) the answer.

5. Aunt Mary (liked, savored) every moment of the time she spent with her niece.

COMMON CORE
STATE STANDARD
L.3.5c

Name_____ Date_____

Shades of Meaning

Draw a line to match each word on the left with its shades of meaning on the right.

1. scared   **a.** shocked, amazed

2. doubt   **b.** thrilled, enthusiastic

3. surprised   **c.** understand, comprehend

4. realize   **d.** drowsy, exhausted

5. tired   **e.** presume, suppose

6. guess   **f.** angry, frustrated

7. excited   **g.** suspect, mistrust

8. assume   **h.** imagine, think

9. upset   **i.** infer, deduce

10. wonder   **j.** terrified, nervous

Common Core Language Grade 3 • ©2014 Newmark Learning, LLC

Name_____ Date_____

COMMON CORE
STATE STANDARD
L.3.5c

Shades of Meaning

Write a sentence to demonstrate the shades of meaning of each word.

1. scared

_____

_____

2. terrified

_____

_____

3. nervous

_____

_____

4. surprised

_____

_____

5. shocked

_____

_____

6. amazed

_____

_____

How to Use the Practice Assessments

The quick practice assessments provided in this section are designed for easy implementation in any classroom. They can be used in several different ways. You may wish to administer a conventions assessment and a vocabulary assessment together. They may also be used individually as an informal assessment tool throughout the year. Use the following charts for item analysis and scoring.

Student Name:

Conventions	Date	Item	Standard	✔=0 X=1	Total
Assessment 1		1	**L.3.1d:** Form and use regular and irregular plural verbs.		
		2	**L.3.2a:** Capitalize appropriate words in titles.		
		3	**L.3.1f:** Ensure subject-verb and pronoun-antecedent agreement.		
		4	**L.3.1h:** Use coordinating and subordinating conjunctions.		
		5	**L.3.1i:** Produce simple, compound, and complex sentences.		
Assessment 2		1	**L.3.1h:** Use coordinating and subordinating conjunctions.		
		2	**L.3.1d:** Form and use regular and irregular verbs.		
		3	**L.3.1g:** Form and use comparative and superlative adjectives and adverbs.		
		4	**L.3.1d:** Form and use regular and irregular verbs.		
		5	**L.3.1h:** Use coordinating and subordinating conjunctions.		
		6	**L.3.1f:** Ensure subject-verb and pronoun-antecedent agreement.		
Assessment 3 Students must rewrite the passage, locating and fixing the five errors.		1	**L.3.2f:** Use spelling patterns and generalizations.		
		2	**L.3.2d:** Form and use possessives.		
		3	**L.3.1b:** Form and use regular and irregular plural nouns.		
		4	**L.3.2c:** Use commas and quotation marks in dialogue.		
		5	**L.3.2d:** Form and use possessives.		
Assessment 4 Students must rewrite the passage, locating and fixing the five errors.		1	**L.3.2f:** Use spelling patterns and generalizations.		
		2	**L.3.2e:** Use conventional spelling for high-frequency and other studied words and for adding suffixes to base words.		
		3	**L.3.1g:** Form and use comparative and superlative adjectives and adverbs.		
		4	**L.3.2c:** Use commas and quotation marks in dialogue.		
		5	**L.3.1h:** Use coordinating and subordinating conjunctions.		

Common Core Language Grade 3 • ©2014 Newmark Learning, LLC

Student Name:

Vocabulary	Date	Item	Standard	✔=0 X=1	Total
Assessment 1		1	**L.3.4d:** Use glossaries dictionaries, both print and digital, to determine or clarify the meaning of words and phrases.		
		2	**L.3.4d:** Use glossaries and dictionaries, both print and digital, to determine or clarify the meaning of words and phrases.		
		3	**L.3.4d:** Use glossaries and dictionaries, both print and digital, to determine or clarify the meaning of words and phrases.		
		4	**L.3.4a:** Use sentence-level context as a clue to the meaning of a word or phrase.		
		5	**L.3.4a:** Use sentence-level context as a clue to the meaning of a word or phrase.		
		6	**L.3.4d:** Use glossaries and dictionaries, both print and digital, to determine or clarify the meaning of words and phrases.		
Assessment 2		1	**L.3.4a:** Use sentence-level context as a clue to the meaning of a word or phrase.		
		2	**L.3.5b:** Identify real-life connections between words and their use.		
		3	**L.3.5c:** Distinguish shades of meaning among related words that describe states of mind or degrees of certainty.		
		4	**L.3.4a:** Use sentence-level context as a clue to the meaning of a word or phrase.		
		5	**L.3.4a:** Use sentence-level context as a clue to the meaning of a word or phrase.		
Assessment 3		1	**L.3.4b:** Determine the meaning of the new word formed when a known affix is added to a known word.		
		2	**L.3.4c:** Use a known root word as a clue to the meaning of an unknown word with the same root.		
		3	**L.3.4c:** Use a known root word as a clue to the meaning of an unknown word with the same root.		
		4	**L.3.4b:** Determine the meaning of the new word formed when a known affix is added to a known word.		
Assessment 4		1	**L.3.5a:** Distinguish literal and nonliteral meanings of words and phrases in context.		
		2	**L.3.5b:** Identify real-life connections between words and their use.		
		3	**L.3.5c:** Distinguish shades of meaning among related words that describe states of mind or degrees of certainty.		
		4	**L.3.5c:** Distinguish shades of meaning among related words that describe states of mind or degrees of certainty.		

COMMON CORE
STATE STANDARDS

L.3.1–
L.3.3

Name_____ Date_____

Read the passage. Then choose the correct form of the underlined sentence.

¹ <u>Grandma shaked Lindsay awake and asked her to help her make a special breakfast for Grandpa.</u> ² <u>Grandma pulled out her old recipe book called the joy of baking.</u> She flipped to the page marked Blueberry Banana Pancakes. Lindsay's eyes lit up. She loves pancakes.

³ <u>Grandma read the recipe aloud to Lindsay, and asked him to get the following ingredients from the cupboard: flour, sugar, salt, and baking powder.</u> ⁴ <u>She grabbed flour, sugar, and salt. She forgot the baking powder.</u> Grandma got the eggs, milk, bananas, and blueberries. Lindsay told Grandma the measurements, and Grandma carefully added the flour, sugar, and salt to the bowl. ⁵ <u>After Lindsay cracked the eggs and poured in the milk, Grandma added the bananas and blueberries to the bowl.</u> As they mixed the pancake batter, Lindsay remembered that she forgot the baking power.

1. Ⓐ Grandma shaked Lindsay awake and asked her to helped her make a special breakfast for Grandpa.

Ⓑ Grandma shake Lindsay awake and asked her to help her make a special breakfast for Grandpa.

Ⓒ Grandma shook Lindsay awake and asked her to help her make a special breakfast for Grandpa.

Ⓓ no change

Common Core Language Grade 3 • ©2014 Newmark Learning, LLC

Name_____ Date_____

2. Ⓐ Grandma pulled out her old recipe book called the Joy of Baking.

Ⓑ Grandma pulled out her old recipe book called the Joy Of Baking.

Ⓒ Grandma pulled out her old recipe book called The Joy of Baking.

Ⓓ no change

3. Ⓐ Grandma read the recipe aloud to Lindsay, and asked her to get the following ingredients from the cupboard: flour, sugar, salt, and baking powder.

Ⓑ Grandma read the recipe aloud to Lindsay, and asked she to get the following ingredients from the cupboard: flour, sugar, salt, and baking powder.

Ⓒ Grandma read the recipe aloud to Lindsay, and asked they to get the following ingredients from the cupboard: flour, sugar, salt, and baking powder.

Ⓓ no change

4. Ⓐ She grabbed flour, sugar, and salt, so forgot the baking powder.

Ⓑ She grabbed flour, sugar, and salt, but she forgot the baking powder.

Ⓒ She grabbed flour, sugar, and salt, or she forgot the baking powder.

Ⓓ no change

5. Ⓐ After Lindsay cracked the eggs. And poured in the milk, Grandma added the bananas and blueberries to the bowl.

Ⓑ After Lindsay cracked the eggs and poured in the milk, yet Grandma added the bananas and blueberries to the bowl.

Ⓒ After Lindsay cracked the eggs and poured in the milk. Grandma added the bananas and blueberries to the bowl.

Ⓓ no change

COMMON CORE
STATE STANDARDS
L.3.1–
L.3.3

Name_____ Date_____

Read the passage. Then choose the correct form of the underlined sentence.

Steven loved helping his dad. [1] Today they were going to check the car over. Because they had to take a long drive to Aunt Lizzie's house on Saturday. First Steven popped the hood by pushing the button inside the car. [2] Then Dad undo the safety latch and open the hood. He pulled out the dipstick to check the oil. Steven gave him a clean cloth to wipe it on and then he dipped it again. [3] He said it was the most blackest oil he had ever seen. Dad said it was time to change it. [4] They could buy oil last night. Steven opened the top of the container for the windshield washer fluid. [5] It was low. Dad helped him pour in more from the jug that was in the trunk. They checked the antifreeze and the brake fluid. Then Dad showed Steven how to check the air pressure in the tires. [6] Steven checked the back tires all by themself. It was fun.

1. Ⓐ Today they were going to check the car over. And they had to take a long drive to Aunt Lizzie's house on Saturday.

   Ⓑ Today they were going to check the car over, so they had to take a long drive to Aunt Lizzie's house on Saturday.

   Ⓒ Today they were going to check the car over, because they had to take a long drive to Aunt Lizzie's house on Saturday.

   Ⓓ no change

Name_____ Date_____

2. Ⓐ Then Dad undone the safety latch and opened the hood.

 Ⓑ Then Dad undid the safety latch and opened the hood.

 Ⓒ Then Dad did not do the safety latch and open the hood.

 Ⓓ no change

3. Ⓐ He said it was the blacker oil he had ever seen.

 Ⓑ He said it was the blackest oil he had ever seen.

 Ⓒ He said it was the most black oil he had ever seen.

 Ⓓ no change

4. Ⓐ They could buy oil yesterday.

 Ⓑ They could buy oil tomorrow.

 Ⓒ They could buy oil two days ago.

 Ⓓ no change

5. Ⓐ It was low, Dad helped him pour in more from the jug that was in the trunk.

 Ⓑ It was low, so Dad helped him poured in more from the jug that was in the trunk.

 Ⓒ It was low. Dad was helping him pour in more from the jug that is in the trunk.

 Ⓓ no change

6. Ⓐ Steven checked the back tires all by himself.

 Ⓑ She checked the back tires all by herself.

 Ⓒ They checked the back tires all by theirself.

 Ⓓ no change

Name_____ Date_____

Read this passage with errors. Underline the errors and then rewrite the passage to fix the errors.

Matt nervisly walked into the locker room. He kept his head down, glancing up every now and again at the others in the room. Matts' locker was number 37. He opened it and put his bag inside. A boy then came over to him.

"Hi, I'm Rory," said the tall boy with black hair. "I am the captain of the team."

"Hi, I'm Matt, and this is my first day of practice," he excitedly said back to Rory. "He then added, I played soccer at my old school in Birmingham Alabama. My team was good. We won the state championships."

Rory smiled and then pointed to the man near the door. He said, "That's the coach. I'll introduce you to him."

Matt thanked Rory and the two boys walked over to the coach. Matt felt more excited than nervous and couldn't wait to get out on the feild.

COMMON CORE
STATE STANDARDS
L.3.1–
L.3.3

Name_____ Date_____

_____

_____

_____

_____

_____

_____

_____

_____

_____

Common Core
State Standards
L.3.1–
L.3.3

Name_____ Date_____

Read this passage with errors. Rewrite the passage to fix the errors.

Chris was surprised to see his sister, Jenna. She was sitting on the front steps. When she saw him, she waved excitedly and leaped to her feet.

"Look what I found on the sidewalk!" she squeeled, waving a box of colored pencils in her brother's face. "Just what I wanted—new art supplies!"

Chris looked thoughtfully at the box. "They are nice pencils," he replyed. "They're better than Aunt Marge's set. In fact, that could be the most goodest set of colored pencils I've ever seen."

Jenna suddenly stopped dancing around. I guess, maybe, keeping them would be greedy "she said sadly." "Whoever lost the pencils is probably upset about it."

Chris nodded. "Put your trust in me, kid," he said. "We'll ask around, find the owner, and return them. I was saving up to buy a new baseball mitt but I think I'd enjoy sharing new colored pencils with you more."

Common Core Language Grade 3 • ©2014 Newmark Learning, LLC

Name_____ Date_____

COMMON CORE
STATE STANDARDS
L.3.1–
L.3.3

_____

_____

_____

_____

_____

_____

_____

_____

_____

_____

Name_____ Date_____

Look at this dictionary entry. Then use it to answer the questions that follow.

tow · er n. 1. a building or structure that is higher than it is long or wide and is higher than its surroundings; 2. a fortress, prison; 3. one that provides support, aid, or protection; 4. a case that holds the parts of a computer. v. 1. to reach or stand high; 2. to rise or surpass others.

ex · plore v. 1. to travel to a new place for adventure or discovery; 2. to carefully look at something in order to understand it; 3. to discuss something in a detailed way; 4. to learn about through experiments or tests.

1. What meaning of **tower** is used in the following sentence?: *In my favorite fairy tale, the princess is trapped in a tower.*

   Ⓐ to reach or stand high

   Ⓑ one that provides support, aid, or protection

   Ⓒ a fortress, prison

   Ⓓ to rise or surpass others

2. Which word would come after the word **tower** in a dictionary?

   Ⓐ town

   Ⓑ towel

   Ⓒ toward

   Ⓓ tour

Name_____ Date_____

3. Which sentence uses the word **tower** correctly as a verb?

(A) Jamal towered into the air and over the steps.

(B) Martin moved the computer tower to the other side of the desk.

(C) She towered off the dishes after she washed them.

(D) Martha towered over the other students in her class.

4. Which sentence uses the word **tower** correctly as a noun?

(A) The Empire State Building towers above many skyscrapers.

(B) The tourist took pictures of the tall tower on the hill.

(C) The truck towered the car to the gas station.

(D) The scared bunny towered in the bushes.

5. What meaning of the word **explore** is used in the following sentence?:
I want to be an astronaut and explore new planets when I grow up.

(A) to learn about through experiments or tests

(B) to carefully look at something in order to understand it

(C) to travel to a new place for adventure or discovery

(D) to discuss something in a detailed way

6. Which word would come after the word **explore** in a dictionary?

(A) explode

(B) export

(C) experiment

(D) explain

COMMON CORE
STATE STANDARDS
**L.3.4–
L.3.6**

Name_____ Date_____

Read the passage. Then answer the questions that follow.

The day was quiet. The wind blew lightly, and all that could be heard was the **rustle** of leaves. Tree branches **swayed** in the breeze. In one of the trees, a nest made of twigs sat upon a **sturdy** tree limb so it would not shake. Three tiny eggs sat inside the nest. The mother **perched** in a tree nearby with her eyes on the nest. Then it happened. One of the eggs began to shake ever so gently. A few cracks formed on the surface of the egg. Then a tiny hole appeared. As the tiny beak poked through the hole, the other two eggs began to shake.

1. What can you determine is happening from the context clues provided in the passage?

    Ⓐ A tree is being cut down.

    Ⓑ A bird is gathering materials to build a nest.

    Ⓒ A storm is on the way.

    Ⓓ A baby bird is hatching from an egg.

Name_____ Date_____

2. The word **rustle** from the passage is a type of

Ⓐ noise

Ⓑ tree

Ⓒ bird

Ⓓ nest

3. What does the word **perched** mean?

Ⓐ to stand on something high

Ⓑ to sleep

Ⓒ to be thirsty

Ⓓ to look closely

4. The word **swayed** means to move side to side. What part of the passage helps you understand what **swayed** means?

Ⓐ in the breeze

Ⓑ Tree branches

Ⓒ the rustle of leaves

Ⓓ a nest made of twigs

5. What does the word **sturdy** mean?

Ⓐ old

Ⓑ big

Ⓒ flimsy

Ⓓ strong

COMMON CORE
STATE STANDARDS
L.3.4–
L.3.6

Name_____ Date_____

Read the passage. Then answer the questions that follow.

Wild animals develop many ways to stay safe from predators, or animals that hunt them. Some animals, like porcupines, have spiky coats that keep predators away. These spikes are called quills. The quills are long and sharp. They stand straight up when the porcupine is scared. Predators soon learn that the quills are very **painful**—and hard to eat! This helps to keep porcupines safe.

Some animals have fur that looks a lot like the environment. This is helpful because the animals blend into their surroundings. It is hard for predators to see them. For example, white-tailed deer are born with a reddish-brown coat with white spots. This coat color looks a lot like the forest around them. The deer seem to **disappear** into the trees. Animals that hunt deer can't always see them.

Other animals develop a colorful skin for **protection**. These animals are **brilliantly** colored and stand out. For example, a poison dart frog's skin is a bright shade of yellow, red, or blue. This coloring makes it easy for other animals to spot the frogs. The bright color sends a signal. It tells predators to stay away. They learn that poison dart frogs are not good to eat and leave these frogs alone.

Common Core Language Grade 3 • ©2014 Newmark Learning, LLC

Name_____ Date_____

COMMON CORE
STATE STANDARDS
L.3.4–
L.3.6

1. Appear means to come into sight. What does **disappear** mean?

Ⓐ before being seen

Ⓑ to stop being seen

Ⓒ to be seen once more

Ⓓ the state of being seen

2. Protect means to keep from harm. What is **protection**?

Ⓐ to feel harm again

Ⓑ the act of causing harm

Ⓒ to cause someone harm

Ⓓ a thing that keeps from harm

3. The word brilliantly comes from the word brilliant. What does **brilliantly** mean?

Ⓐ in a bright manner

Ⓑ without brightness

Ⓒ the opposite of bright

Ⓓ something that makes brightness

4. The word pain means hurt or suffering. What does the word **painful** mean?

Ⓐ without hurt

Ⓑ to hurt more

Ⓒ full of pain

Ⓓ one who causes hurt

Common Core
State Standards
L.3.4–
L.3.6

Name_____ Date_____

Read the passage. Then answer the questions that follow.

America is a democracy. This is a type of government that fully involves the people. The Founding Fathers wanted to make sure the government was always a democracy. They took steps to make this happen. Instead, they wrote a document called the Constitution. This document set out a specific plan for government.

The Constitution divides the government into three branches. The Founding Fathers believed this would stop any one person or group from getting too much power. The three branches are the legislative branch, the executive branch, and the judicial branch.

The legislative branch is called Congress. They are a group of 535 people who make drafts of laws, called bills. The executive branch is mainly the president. The president chooses which bills become laws. The president also chooses who is in the judicial branch.

The judicial branch is called the Supreme Court. The Supreme Court is a group of nine judges, called justices. They have the power to abolish any law they think is unfair.

Common Core Language Grade 3 • ©2014 Newmark Learning, LLC

Name_____ Date_____

1. Based on the passage, which of the following *best* gives the meaning of "took steps"?

   Ⓐ walked up stairs

   Ⓑ measures taken to achieve a goal

   Ⓒ removed a ledge or stairway

   Ⓓ moved feet in a particular pattern, danced

2. Based on the passage, which word *best* describes the Founding Fathers?

   Ⓐ afraid

   Ⓑ selfish

   Ⓒ thoughtful

   Ⓓ cheerful

3. Pick the word that best completes the sentence.
   The Founding Fathers _____ democracy was a good idea.

   Ⓐ thought

   Ⓑ suspected

   Ⓒ believed

   Ⓓ imagined

4. Pick the word that best completes the sentence.
   When people vote for the president, they must _____ he or she is the best person for the job.

   Ⓐ feel

   Ⓑ think

   Ⓒ imagine

   Ⓓ believe

Answer Key, pages 7–19

page 7

1. thing	2. place	3. person
4. place	5. thing	6. place
7. thing	8. thing	9. person
10. person		

page 8

1. grandfather, flowers
2. teacher, name, chalkboard
3. flute
4. fish, bowl
5. Mom, Uncle Hank's
6. Oreo, Jess
7. Dad's, Boston
8. Leo, Texas

page 10

1. She   2. They   3. it   4. them

page 11

1. The baby bird opened its beak when its mother flew into the nest.
2. My friend Angela wants to wear her new coat to the football game tonight.
3. Nick and Tommy like to ride their bikes each day after school.
4. Mr. Antonio gave each of his students a box of crayons for an art project.

page 13

1. listened	2. soared
3. play	4. laughs, tells
5. dashed	6. eat
7. wrestled	8. cooked

page 14

(sample answers shown)

1. tastes	2. are	3. looks
4. smell	5. feels	6. is
7. ran	8. tastes	9. sang
10. dug		

page 16

1. The (red) bird perched at the top of the tree.
2. My (lazy) sister Ray likes to sleep until noon.
3. The boy with the (black) hair is Kevin.
4. The baby shook the rattle in its (tiny) hand.
5. Ask Paul to tell us a (funny) story.
6. We sat on a (soft) blanket because we did not want to sit on the (wet) grass.
7. The textbook for class was (heavy.)
8. The (little) dog played with his (squeaky) toy.

page 17

Answers may vary for the adjective web.

Our hamster Charlie has <u>long</u>, <u>curly</u> fur. Charlie likes to sleep in the <u>soft</u> bedding in his <u>large</u> cage. When he is not napping, he likes to run in a <u>big</u>, <u>purple</u> wheel. He also likes to crawl through the <u>long</u> tunnels in his cage. As a <u>special</u> treat, we feed him <u>juicy</u> carrots and <u>sweet</u> cereal. Charlie is a <u>wonderful</u> pet.

page 19

1. She <u>looked</u> at the bowl of fruit (hungrily.)
2. Phillip <u>searched</u> for his baseball mitt (outside.)
3. He <u>rubbed</u> his eyes (sleepily.)

Answer Key, pages 19–27

(page 19 continued)

4. Dad <u>left</u> for work (early.)

5. The door <u>closed</u> (loudly.)

6. Amy (gently) <u>set</u> the glass vase down on the table.

7. Ming <u>filled</u> his plate (greedily) with cookies.

8. They <u>played</u> games (inside) during the thunderstorm.

page 20

1. gracefully
2. neatly
3. high
4. softly
5. carefully, here
6. steadily
7. patiently
8. inside, heavily
9. first
10. accidentally

page 21

1. (Aaron) went to the (movies) with <u>his</u> (brother)(Phil.)

2. <u>My</u> (mom) went to see a (play) in (New York City.)

3. (Jacinda) forget to grab <u>her</u> (purse) when <u>she</u> left the (house.)

4. (Ralph) went (upstairs) so <u>he</u> could play (games) with <u>his</u> (brother.)

5. The (brothers) walked to the (bus stop) around the (corner) and <u>they</u> waited for the (bus.)

6. asked, wash
7. is
8. took
9. dug
10. placed

The <u>loud</u> chef works in a <u>busy</u> restaurant (nightly.) The <u>hot</u> kitchen is (very)(tiny.) There is <u>little</u> room to move. (Sometimes) plates of <u>hot</u> food are dropped on the <u>dirty</u> floor (accidentally.) When this happens, the <u>angry</u> chef has to remake the <u>delicious</u> dishes.

page 23

1. daughters
2. flashes
3. patches
4. tomatoes
5. valleys
6. buzzes
7. flowers
8. robes
9. telephones
10. heroes

page 24

1. <u>hammers</u>, <u>handles</u>
2. <u>ribbons</u>, <u>races</u>
3. <u>boxes</u>, <u>gifts</u>
4. <u>kittens</u>, <u>bugs</u>
5. <u>sisters</u>, <u>beaches</u>
6. <u>sandwiches</u>, <u>tables</u>
7. <u>rabbits</u>, <u>hutches</u>
8. <u>eggs</u>, <u>potatoes</u>, <u>dinners</u>

page 25

(sample answers shown)

1. I got new <u>glasses</u>.
2. The hairdresser had many <u>brushes</u>.
3. I read about <u>heroes</u> in comic books.
4. Many farms have <u>turkeys</u>.
5. <u>Foxes</u> run through the woods.

page 26

1. berries
2. lives
3. ponies
4. loaves
5. calves
6. skies
7. wives
8. strawberries

page 27

1. Jack believed he saw <u>elves</u>.
2. The boy ran from the <u>wolves</u>.
3. The goose ate <u>blueberries</u>.

Answer Key, pages 27–36

(page 27 continued)

4. Paki cut the <u>loaves</u> of bread with <u>knives</u>.

5. Kara watched the horse lift its <u>hooves</u> for the blacksmith.

page 28

(sample answers shown)

1. Put the books on the <u>shelves</u>.

2. The <u>thieves</u> stole valuable jewelry.

3. Cut the pie into <u>halves</u>.

4. The orange <u>leaves</u> are beautiful.

5. Chefs use different <u>knives</u>.

page 29

1. donkeys   2. lives   3. juices

4. worms   5. flies   6. pianos

7. spoons   8. princesses   9. hooves

10. monkeys

(sample answers shown)

1. My <u>feet</u> hurt after running.

2. The <u>elves</u> are so cute.

3. My <u>cousins</u> live in Michigan.

4. We ate <u>sandwiches</u> for lunch.

page 31

Answers may vary.

page 32

(sample answers shown)

1. I started a <u>friendship</u> with my new neighbor.

2. <u>Anger</u> can cause many problems in the classroom.

3. The knight was rewarded for his <u>bravery</u> in battle.

(page 32 continued)

4. Having a big <u>imagination</u> is a special trait.

5. Aaron's <u>honesty</u> allowed him to get voted class president.

6. When my mom asked if I had broken her lamp, I decided to tell her the <u>truth</u>.

page 33

(sample answers shown)

1. Seek *knowledge* and wisdom.

2. Life's simple *joys* are worth sharing.

3. The children felt *satisfaction* while swimming on a hot summer day.

4. The puppy satisfied her *curiosity* by chasing the squirrel.

5. greed: He looked at the pile of money with greed in his eyes.

6. truth: You should speak the truth.

page 35

1. watched   2. begged   3. called

4. dragged   5. carried

6. surprised   7. drifted   8. poked

9. tried   10. picked

page 36

(sample answers shown)

1. The sailor <u>floated</u> down the river in his tiny boat.

2. I <u>hugged</u> my dog after I returned from sleepaway camp.

3. A new student <u>named</u> Greg joined our classroom today.

4. My older brother <u>poked</u> me with a stick.

Answer Key, pages 36–45

(page 36 continued)

5. The box full of books was too heavy to carry, so I <u>pushed</u> it across the floor.

6. I <u>crawled</u> under my bed while playing hide-and-seek.

page 37

1. I scrubbed my face every morning.

2. The seeds sprouted in the flowerpot.

3. Beth passed the carrots at the dinner table.

4. The plane landed on the runway.

5. The ice melted on the sidewalk.

6. Sandra boiled the water and poured the tea.

page 38

1. chose	2. drank	3. kept
4. lost	5. caught	6. threw
7. gave	8. rose	9. blew
10. built	11. wrote	12. read
13. swung	14. led	15. made
16. left	17. paid	18. spread
19. stung	20. swam	

page 39

1. spent	2. stood	3. did
4. drove	5. ate	6. paid
7. rode	8. took	9. shook
10. said	11. won	12. rode
13. wound	14. stuck	15. saw
16. broke		

page 40

1. grew	2. left	3. stood
4. fell	5 held	6. flew

page 41

(sample answers shown)

1. We <u>ate</u> dinner.

2. They <u>sat</u> over there.

3. I <u>heard</u> a strange noise.

4. She <u>paid</u> the bill.

5. They <u>rode</u> their bikes.

6. He <u>drank</u> coffee after dinner.

page 43

1. Juan studied for the science test.

2. We drove to the store and shopped for new sneakers.

3. Maria wrote a letter to her best friend.

4. My sister sang a song in the talent show.

(sample answer shown)

I went outside and played basketball for two hours.

page 44

I heard a noise coming from the basement. I crept slowly down the stairs. I thought it was just the washing machine, but I was really not sure. There was a big thumping noise. It repeated over and over. It sounded like a giant heartbeat. I reached the last step. I closed my eyes and turned the corner. The thumping noise was getting louder. Then I laughed. I saw my dog. He was standing next to the dryer and his wagging tail banged against the dryer door.

page 45

1. look	2. says	3. waits
4. rides	5. gets	6. barks

Answer Key, pages 46–58

page 46

1. Benny always wears green because it is his favorite color.
2. Rita is brushing her dog's long fur coat.
3. When we are quiet, Mr. Clark gives us free time.
4. She rides the bus to school in the morning.
5. Lars seems sure of the answer.
6. The birds sing sweetly in the flower garden.

page 47

1. will pick
2. will see
3. will watch
4. will play
5. will be
6. will travel
7. will drive
8. will leave
9. will drink
10. will say

page 48

1. We will cook dinner over a campfire.
2. She will return her library books.
3. Tita will bake muffins for the children.
4. He will build a model plane.
5. Saturday I will clean my room.
6. I will go to the grocery store to get milk.

page 49

1. will travel
2. won
3. go
4. was
5. started
6. wait

page 51

1. steals
2. hop
3. eat, wash
4. asks
5. wander
6. lose

page 52

(sample answers shown)

1. ran
2. drink
3. pretend
4. wakes
5. sings
6. tasted
7. grow
8. started
9. closes
10. practices

page 53

(sample answers shown)

1. they
2. her
3. he
4. our
5. their
6. she
7. he
8. his

page 54

1. their
2. its
3. she, her
4. his
5. we
6. he
7. I, my
8. it
9. his
10. their
11. her
12. our

page 55

1. swims
2. enjoys
3. feel
4. walks
5. roast
6. their
7. it
8. them
9. his
10. they

page 57

1. best
2. most quickly
3. prettiest
4. least dangerous
5. worst
6. tallest
7. biggest
8. happiest

page 58

1. greener, greenest
2. more open, most open
3. more beautiful, most beautiful

Answer Key, pages 58–67

(page 58 continued)

4. earlier, earliest

5. closer, closest

6. happier, happiest

7. finer, finest

page 59

(sample answers shown)

1. She is <u>taller</u> than me.

2. It's <u>hotter</u> in here than out there.

3. Let's climb <u>higher</u>!

4. The sky is <u>bluer</u> than yesterday.

5. That is the <u>lowest</u> level.

6. She is the <u>best</u> dog.

7. This food is the <u>worst</u>.

8. I'm the <u>happiest</u> I'll ever be.

page 60

1. more beautifully   2. harder

3. farther   4. most graceful

5. longest

page 61

1. more sadly, most sadly

2. more slowly, most slowly

3. more quietly, most quietly

4. more warmly, most warmly

5. farther, farthest

6. sooner, soonest

7. more carefully, most carefully

page 62

1. earlier   2. more ferociously

3. more rapidly   4. best

(page 62 continued)

5. most correctly   6. more frequently

7. hardest   8. more carefully

page 63

<u>Comparative</u>: quieter, easier, angrier, less, heavier, worse, better, shorter, prettier, simpler

<u>Superlative</u>: shortest, least, fastest, best, simplest, worst

page 65

1. I can't go to the pool today, and I can't go to the pool tomorrow.

2. Should Gina buy a juice, or should she eat an orange?

3. My sister wants to see a movie, so she will buy a paper to check the show times.

page 66

1. Will the game end in a tie, <u>or</u> will it go into overtime?

2. The cake looked beautiful, <u>but</u> few people ate it.

3. The snow stopped falling, <u>so</u> we took our sleds outside.

4. Gina measured the flour, <u>and</u> her mother cracked the eggs.

5. Dad couldn't find his keys, <u>but</u> Mom found them in his jacket pocket.

6. I had a science test, <u>so</u> I studied.

page 67

(sample answers shown)

1. I will pick you up at 5 o'clock, however I might be late.

2. We climbed the stairs because we found an artist painting at the window.

Answer Key, pages 67–77

(page 67 continued)

3. Ingrid went to the door when she heard the buzzer.

page 68

Answers may vary.

page 69

Answers may vary.

page 71

2, 3, 7, 8

page 72

1. (Mother) passed the salt to father.

2. (Tyrell) makes funny faces in the mirror.

3. (The plane) landed smoothly on the runway.

4. (The hawk) soars high in the clear sky.

5. (The pirate) buried the treasure.

(sample answers shown)

6. The canary sang a beautiful song.

7. Christina is my best friend.

8. We studied for the test.

9. Alex went down the water slide.

page 73

1. I brushed my teeth, and I went to bed.

2. Manny likes fruit pie, but Rita likes cream pie.

3. Do you want to watch a movie, or do you want to play outside?

4. The hammer is used to hit nails, and the ax is used to chop wood.

page 74

1. (The leaves) change colors, and (they) fall off the trees in autumn.

2. (Julie) packed her suitcase, and (she) flew on a plane.

3. (Orange) is my favorite color, but (yellow) is my least favorite color.

4. (The boys) cleaned the garage, so (Dad) took them to the park.

5. (The class) went to the zoo, and (they) learned about different animals.

Answers may vary.

page 75

1. although he does not know how to swim.

2. Even though the necklace is pretty,

3. After the chef added the flour,

4. when Ted opens the door.

5. because they were going sailing.

6. After the farmer plowed the fields,

page 76

1. the sun is in the sky.

2. Susie yelled at her little sister

3. he gave out homework.

4. David's mom drove him to school

5. she also enjoys basketball.

Answers may vary.

page 77

1. simple   2. complex

3. compound   4. complex

5. simple   6. compound

7. complex   8. complex

9. simple   10. compound

Answer Key, pages 79–89

page 79

1. Tales of a Fourth Grade Nothing
2. The Legend of Sleepy Hollow
3. The Wonderful Wizard of Oz
4. The Adventures of Tom Sawyer
5. Anne of Green Gables
6. A Wrinkle in Time

page 80

1. Through the Looking-Glass
2. Mrs. Doubtfire
3. Harry Potter and the Chamber of Secrets
4. Thunder Birds: Nature's Flying Predators
5. Kit Kittredge: An American Girl

page 81

1. c   2. b   3. c   4. a   5. b   6. b

page 83

3, 5

page 84

1. My brother attends Harvard University in Cambridge, Massachusetts.
2. William Getty, 33 Juniper Place, Detroit, MI 48201
3. Regina Herman, 60511 Station Boulevard, Biloxi, MS 39530
4. Kareem Greene, 888 Whispering Pines Lane, Saint Paul, MN 55104
5. I want to go on vacation in San Francisco, California.
6. Uncle Arthur likes to fish in Sitka, Alaska, in the winter months.

(page 84 continued)

7. Jessica Lewis-Day, 75 North Red Rock Street, Denver, CO 80022
8. The beaches in Cape May, New Jersey, are beautiful.

page 85

1. a   2. c   3. c   4. b   5. b

page 87

1. a   2. c   3. a

page 88

1. The excited boy yelled to his grandmother, "I see it! I see it!"
2. The babysitter said to the children, "Who wants to go to the park today?"
3. "It won't be too much longer now until the doctor will see you," said the nurse to the patient.
4. Alice nervously recited from the stage, "Jack and Jill went up the hill."
5. He picked up the phone and said, "Hello. This is Mr. Weaver. How can I help you?"
6. She looked at her sister and asked, "Are you wearing my shirt to school today?"
7. My mom gave me a big hug and said, "You were so great in the play! I am so proud."
8. "What would you like for dinner tonight?" my dad asked.

page 89

1. The doctor asked the little girl, "How are you feeling?"
2. She sang the lyrics, "You are my sunshine, my only sunshine."

Answer Key, pages 89–98

(page 89 continued)

3. "Hurry along, and have a safe day," the crossing guard said to the students.

4. "You have a choice between salad and broccoli today," said the lunch lady to the hungry little boy.

5. Mr. White asked, "Who is ready for a pop quiz?"

Answers may vary.

page 91

1. Ms. Smith's groceries
2. his father's shovel
3. Mr. Hess's car
4. her sister's scooter
5. roosters' crowing
6. children's cries

page 92

1. Rita's books
2. people's choice
3. Today's winner
4. Julia's old skates
5. father's garage
6. actors' costumes
7. Maria's hair
8. class's homework

page 93

1. the boy's ice cream
2. the frogs' croaking
3. Tomas's notebook
4. the children's answer
5. the mice's squeaking
6. the cat's whiskers
7. Lana's mittens
8. Ross's pencil

page 95

1. eight	2. try	3. about
4. light	5. laugh	6. myself
7. really	8. can't	9. please
10. because	11. would	12. today
13. these	14. own	
15. together	16. clean	17. their
18. only	19. wash	20. right

page 96

1. Liam <u>heard</u> the <u>sound</u> of the <u>fountain</u> in the <u>garden</u>.
2. The third grade <u>teacher</u> <u>checked</u> each student's homework.
3. Gary <u>turned</u> off the lights to save <u>energy</u>.
4. <u>Tomorrow</u> we will <u>practice</u> <u>fractions</u> in school.
5. We <u>followed</u> along as Ms. Farrel <u>checked</u> our <u>answers</u>.

page 97

1. prepared, preparing
2. hugged, hugging
3. raised, raising
4. noisier, noisiest, noisily
5. grander, grandest, grandly
6. closer, closest, closely

page 98

1. welcomed, welcoming
2. belonged, belonging
3. flowed, flowing
4. bigger, biggest
5. hotter, hottest
6. redder, reddest
7. fiercest, fiercely
8. blindest, blindly
9. freshest, freshly

Answer Key, pages 99–109

page 99

1. calmly
2. teary
3. playfully
4. latest
5. collecting
6. rainy
7. begging
8. higher
9. biggest
10. laughed
11. juicy
12. lighter

page 101

1. The <u>moon</u> <u>rose</u> in the <u>night</u> sky.
2. The <u>catcher</u> <u>caught</u> the <u>first</u> <u>pitch</u>.
3. Lisa <u>likes</u> to <u>splash</u> in the <u>pool</u> on hot days.
4. The <u>kite</u> <u>climbed</u> <u>higher</u> as we raced <u>through</u> the park.
5. Laura <u>wrapped</u> the <u>scarf</u> around her <u>neck</u>.
6. The lion <u>yawned</u> in its <u>cage</u> and <u>licked</u> its <u>whiskers</u>.

page 102

1. We <u>drive</u> <u>near</u> the <u>library</u> <u>when</u> we visit <u>our</u> <u>Aunt</u> Annie.
2. <u>Please</u> <u>wrap</u> the <u>sandwiches</u> in <u>foil</u>.
3. The <u>flight</u> was <u>late</u> so Maria waited at the airport.
4. I will give this <u>note</u> to your <u>teacher</u>.
5. Tony <u>squeezed</u> the water out of the <u>soapy</u> <u>sponges</u>.
6. The wind <u>roared</u> and <u>rocked</u> the boat.
7. Mimi steered her bicycle <u>around</u> the obstacle <u>course</u>.
8. Nina's <u>favorite</u> color is <u>blue</u>.
9. Dan fills his mug to the <u>brim</u> with warm milk every <u>night</u>.
10. We <u>knew</u> Brian <u>would</u> <u>play</u> baseball today.

page 103

1. leans
2. might
3. landed
4. wrinkles
5. laugh

6–10: Answers may vary.

page 105

1. butterfly
2. famous
3. (correct)
4. curtain
5. seventy
6. (correct)
7. honor
8. (correct)
9. receive
10. lonely

page 106

1. desert
2. fur
3. pitcher
4. nap
5. hospital

Answers may vary.

page 107

1. plane <no>
2. peddler <yes>
3. parent <yes>
4. pack <no>
5. paid <no>
6. pencil <yes>
7. pour <no>
8. president <no>
9. pilot <yes>
10. piano <yes>
11. received
12. interesting
13. different
14. believe
15. really (correct)
16. always

page 109

Students should circle descriptive words and phrases in the passage.

1. thin (spare, slim, lean)
2. very (quite, awfully, extremely)
3. dog (husky, terrier, boxer)
4. walk (march, skip, tramp)

Answer Key, pages 110—123

page 110

Answers may vary.

page 111

Answers may vary.

page 113

The main character in this book is Milly, a cat who wants to be a detective. She follows her owner, a mail carrier named Harley, around town. When someone starts to steal packages that Harley has delivered, Milly is on the case. She asks other cats and even some mice for help. Milly makes sure Harley sees the clues she finds. Harley thinks he solves the case, but Milly is the real detective. The author describes their friendship well and makes the story interesting and exciting.

page 114

Dear Uncle Martin,

We're having a great time camping. Thanks for suggesting the idea. The first thing we did yesterday was go hiking through a pine forest. The forest was full of birds.

We cook over a campfire at night. After dinner we sat, talked, and looked at the sky. Tomorrow we're going to try rowing. Mom said she will teach me.

Thanks for loaning us your tent. I like having my own room. We'll see you next week.

Love, Taylor

page 115

1. Molly wrote her book report while eating a sandwich.

2. Dan returned his books to the library.

3. Lina's little sister makes faces when her dad takes photos.

4. Turn on/off the lights.

5. Because of the heavy rain, we held the meeting inside.

6. His older sister may bring us home after the show.

7. Dina went to the new park to see what it was like.

8. Harry's brother adores the kittens.

page 116

Answers may vary.

page 119

1. fixed

2. whined, cried, grumbled

3. confused, uncertain

4. floated, coasted, flowed

5. cry, wail

page 120

1. a   2. b   3. a   4. b   5. a

page 121

1. starving   2. delicate   3. pleasant
4. kneaded   5. brilliant   6. irate

Answers may vary.

page 123

1. un—not safe   2. re—build again

3. mis—treat wrongly   4. pre—cook before

5. un—not able   6. un—not stick

7. re—think again   8. re—fill again

9. mis—spell wrong   10. mis—wrong place

176

Answer Key, pages 124—135

page 124

1. predawn
2. refasten
3. prepackaged
4. reuse
5. misbehave
6. unhealthy
7. mislead
8. unpainted
9. uneven
10. misunderstood
11. refill
12. unfair
13. preschool

page 125

1. taller—more tall
2. wonderful—extremely good
3. smartest—most intelligent
4. beautiful—good-looking
5. loudest—most loud
6. fearless—having no fear
7. boastful
8. darkest
9. colder
10. helpless
11. bolder
12. wildest
13. faithful
14. careless

page 126

1. without color
2. full of care
3. most high
4. full of truth
5. without spots
6. more wide

Answers may vary.

page 127

1. shirtless
2. colorful
3. unfair
4. misbehaves
5. helpful
6. powerless
7. reuse
8. unpainted
9. pretest
10. redo

page 129

1. hang
2. forget
3. thought
4. behave
5. weak
6. button
7. big
8. wish
9. heat
10. beauty

page 130

1. without use
2. full of harm
3. not worn
4. more lively
5. doesn't trust
6. most thin
7. full plate
8. cook before

page 131

1. unhappy
2. misguide
3. repack
4. precook

Answers may vary.

5. careless
6. stranger
7. smartest
8. peaceful

Answers may vary.

page 133

1. snow
2. thunder
3. lightning
4. rain

page 134

1. a person who flies a plane
2. a group of animals
3. to cut or separate into two or more parts
4. the flower of a plant
5. a way, road, or course of travel
6. a large meal

page 135

1. b   2. f   3. h   4. a   5. d
6. j   7. i   8. c   9. e   10. g

Answer Key, pages 137–147

page 137

1. nonliteral (best)
2. literal (by her sides)
3. literal (climbed, to watch)
4. nonliteral (about going)
5. nonliteral (for missing practice)
6. literal (carrots, to cook)
7. nonliteral (cause trouble)
8. literal (running around)

page 138

1. literal
2. nonliteral
3. literal
4. nonliteral
5. nonliteral
6. literal
7. nonliteral
8. literal
9. nonliteral
10. literal

page 139

1. give me a hand
2. step on it
3. drew a blank
4. lent a hand
5. down in the dumps
6. in hot water

Answers may vary.

page 141

Answers may vary.

page 142

1. easy, understand
2. sleepy, distracted
3. ball, Earth
4. soup, milkshake, applesauce
5. gum, candy, honey

(page 142 continued)

6. joke, laughed
7. red, hot, dropped her books in front of…
8. butterfly, daisy

page 143

Answers may vary.

page 145

1. pound
2. boasted
3. snapped
4. knew
5. savored

page 146

1. j   2. g   3. a   4. c   5. d
6. i   7. b   8. e   9. f   10. h

page 147

Answers may vary.

1. The noise scared the chipmunk, and it ran up the tree.
2. She was terrified when she saw a spider.
3. Jamal was nervous the bus would leave without him.
4. Mariah was surprised by her friend's answer.
5. Bill was shocked that Sharon agreed to go to the dance with him.
6. The parents were amazed when their daughter won first place in the spelling bee.

Common Core Language Grade 3 • ©2014 Newmark Learning, LLC

Answer Key, pages 150–165

Assessment Answers

pages 150–151

1. C   2. C   3. A   4. B   5. D

pages 152–153

1. C   2. B   3. B   4. B   5. D   6. A

pages 154–155

Matt <u>nervously</u> walked into the locker room. He kept his head down, glancing up every now and again at the others in the room<u>. Matt's</u> locker was number 37.

He opened it and put his bag inside. A boy then came over to him.

"Hi, I'm Rory," said the tall boy with black hair. "I am the captain of the team."

"Hi, I'm Matt, and this is my first day of practice," he excitedly said back to Rory. <u>He then added, "I</u> played soccer at my old school in <u>Birmingham, Alabama.</u> My team was good. We won the state championships."

Rory smiled and then pointed to the man near the door. He said, "That's the coach. I'll introduce you to him."

Matt thanked Rory and the two boys walked over to the coach. Matt felt more excited than nervous and couldn't wait to get out on the <u>field</u>.

pages 156–157

Chris was surprised to see his sister, Jenna, sitting on the front steps. When she saw him, she waved excitedly and leaped to her feet.

"Look what I found on the sidewalk!" she <u>squealed,</u> waving a box of colored pencils in her brother's face. "Just what I wanted—new art supplies!"

(pages 156–157 continued)

Chris looked thoughtfully at the box. "They are nice pencils," he <u>replied</u>. "They're better than Aunt Marge's set. In fact, that could be the <u>best</u> set of colored pencils I've ever seen."

Jenna suddenly stopped dancing around. <u>"I guess, maybe, keeping them would be greedy,"</u> she said sadly. "Whoever lost the pencils is probably upset about it."

Chris nodded. "Put your trust in me, kid," he said. "We'll ask around, find the owner, and return them. I was saving up to buy a new baseball <u>mitt, but</u> I think I'd enjoy sharing new colored pencils with you more."

pages 158–159

1. C   2. A   3. D   4. B   5. C   6. B

pages 160–161

1. D   2. A   3. A   4. A   5. D

pages 162–163

1. B   2. D   3. A   4. C

pages 164–165

1. B   2. C   3. C   4. D

Notes

_____

_____

_____

_____

_____

_____

_____

_____

_____

_____

_____

_____